Dwight L. Carlson M.D.

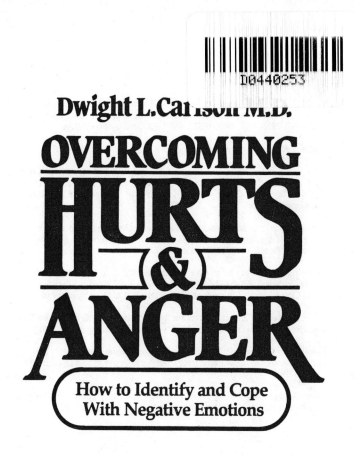

# OVERCOMING
# HURTS
# (&)
# ANGER

## How to Identify and Cope With Negative Emotions

**HARVEST HOUSE PUBLISHERS**
Eugene, Oregon 97402

## OVERCOMING HURTS AND ANGER

*With affection to Susan and Greg,
my dear children.*

# CONTENTS

Preface

# Preface

As a practicing internist for ten years and now as a practicing psychiatrist for five, I have had the opportunity to care for thousands of patients with every conceivable physical and emotional symptom. They have been people from every walk of life, from every social stratum, and from every religious background. One of the most common causes of their symptoms has been the inability to sense their feelings of hurt, along with their resultant anger and their inability to deal with these feelings constructively.

Many of the emotional problems of the world would be solved if the principles of this book were properly applied. In many individuals, virtually all their psychological problems would be eradicated by the application of the contents of these pages.

There are several viewpoints on how to deal with anger. At one extreme is the currently popular emphasis of giving full vent to one's anger.

Psychologists have become increasingly aware of the harmful, long-term effects of repressing anger, so many of them now advocate expressing anger rather than bottling it up, even if expressing it hurts others. Drs. Back and Goldberg seem to be promoting this viewpoint in their book *Creative Aggression*.

At the other extreme is the view that anger is wrong, and that, therefore, one should be totally passive, a sort of human doormat. I believe that Albert Ellis' *How to Live With and Without Anger* is an example of this approach. He says, "...we consider virtually all anger at a person inappropriate" (page 73).

In my opinion, neither of these approaches deals adequately and constructively with anger.

This book presents what I believe to be a balanced approach to the subject, and offers guidelines that can help you deal with hurt and anger in ways that are least likely to adversely affect you or those around you.

It has been my experience that someone who handles anger properly is a mature, whole person, capable of giving and receiving love. The knowledge and insights shared in this book come not only out of a sound psychological framework, but I believe are consistent with the Bible, which is a vitally important guideline for myself and for many readers. Therefore, while the Christians will hopefully find the principles in this book to be consistent with their beliefs, I believe that non-Christians will also find the methods taught for handling anger to be useful even though they may not agree with the theological position. In fact, I have used the principles in this book with individuals of varied religious persuasions and have found them to be consistently effective.

All the things which I discuss in the following pages are things that I have personally wrestled with in my own life, and have seen work in scores of my patients. Thus, this book comes not only out of a theoretical framework, but also out of practical experience, both personal and professional.

All the examples used in this book are true, but names and incidental features have been altered sufficiently to preserve the privacy of the individuals involved.

I want to thank Rev. Rueben M. Baerg for reviewing the manuscript and, in particular, the scriptural application.

I greatly appreciate the tremendous assistance in typing and editing by my wife, Betty, and my niece, Lynette Carlson.

*—Dwight L. Carlson*

# Chapter

# One

## *The Many Faces of Anger*

### Misconceptions About Anger

Jan is an attractive college sophomore who stood several months ago on top of the Vincent Thomas Bridge in San Pedro, California, and seriously contemplated jumping. Several weeks ago she attempted suicide by taking an overdose of pills.

Today she sat in my office, ready for this week's psychotherapy session. Jan started by telling me about an event that happened Thursday afternoon. She said she felt funny and confused, and walked aimlessly around the campus and the adjacent shopping mall. This confusion lasted for several hours, and then she returned to her dorm and felt better. "That was it," she said, "That's all!"

"You mean you had this episode of aimless confusion for several hours and that's what was troubling you?" I asked.

"Yes," she said.

I waited for more, but all I got was silence. I asked about further feelings or precipitating factors that might have happened that day. Still she came up with nothing. She had had no other feelings, and nothing unusual had happened during that previous 24 hours. Already 20 minutes of the session had passed, and we seemed to be making little progress.

Eventually I asked, "What do you normally do on Thursday afternoon around 2:30?"

She replied that she normally went to her chemistry class.

"So you didn't attend class Thursday?" I questioned.

"No," she answered. When I asked her why, she didn't seem to know.

Because I knew that Jan was very conscientious and that this was highly unusual behavior for her, I questioned her further. Eventually I found out that in the previous chemistry class her lab partner was having trouble understanding the instructions, so Jan was trying to help by quietly explaining them. But the instructor heard the whispering and snapped, "Be quiet, Jan." Jan instantly quieted down and didn't say another word the rest of the class.

When I asked her how she felt about the instructor's remark, she at first denied having any reaction or feeling anything. But as I probed further and pointed out that there must have been a powerful reason why she didn't attend class, she finally was able to get in touch with a slight feeling of irritation at the teacher.

You see, one of Jan's basic problems is that she is a very sensitive person who has been led to believe that all anger is wrong. For about the last four years she had progressively hidden from herself her own feeling of irritation and anger. This powerful source of energy had become repressed to such a degree that she literally felt nothing. Even when she was ready to jump off the bridge, she said she felt "numb". When people would insult her, she wouldn't feel hurt or angry, but on the other hand, when something good happened, she wasn't able to feel happy either.

Jan illustrates Misconception #1 that many people have about anger: *If you don't look, feel, or seem angry, you don't have an anger problem.*

Missionary Joseph Cooke tells how he tried to suppress his anger in his book *Free for the Taking* (pp. 109-10):

> . . . squelching our feelings never pays. In fact, it's rather like plugging up a steam vent

in a boiler. When the steam is stopped in one place, it will come out somewhere else. Either that or the whole business will blow up in your face. And bottled-up feelings are just the same. If you bite down your anger, for example, it often comes out in another form that is much more difficult to deal with. It changes into sullenness, self-pity, depression, or snide, cutting remarks . . . .

Not only may bottled-up emotions come out sideways in various unpleasant forms; they also may build up pressure until they simply have to burst forth. And when they do, someone is almost bound to get hurt . . . .

I remember that for years and years of my . . . life, I worked to bring my emotions under control. Over and over again, as they cropped up, I would master them in my attempt to achieve what looked like a gracious, imperturbable Christian spirit. Eventually, I had nearly everybody fooled, even in a measure my own wife. But it was all a fake. I had a nice-looking outward appearance; but inside, there was almost nothing there . . . .

And way underneath, almost completely beyond the reach of my conscious mind, the mass of feelings lay bottled up. I didn't even know they were there myself, except when their pale ghosts would surface now and then in various kinds of unsanctified attitudes and reactions. But they were nevertheless. And the time came when the whole works blew up in my face, in an emotional breakdown.

All the things that had been buried so long came out in the open. Frankly, there was no healing, no recovery, no building a new life for me until all those feelings were sorted out, and until I learned to know them for what they were, accept them, and find some way of expressing them honestly and nondestructively.

In my opinion, he fell victim to Misconception #2: *If you ignore your hurts and anger, they will go away and won't cause you any trouble later on.*

Joe is a 26-year-old machinist. One thing is sure—he doesn't have any trouble expressing his feelings. He makes it quite clear when he is angry—a little *too* clear. Everyone was quite aware of the fact that he was angry when he broke his guitar into a thousand pieces just because his friend criticized his playing. His son knew he was angry at him for leaving his bike in the driveway, because Joe deliberately drove over the back wheel of the bike. His wife is very aware of his anger when he breaks windows, doors, dishes, and furniture.

Joe is applying the theory currently in vogue that says that if you just get your feelings and anger out in the open, you'll feel better and everything will be fine. But there's just one problem with this view—it doesn't always work. At least it doesn't work for Joe, who is miserable and frequently on the brink of suicide. He has fallen prey to the tempting Misconception #3: *Just let all your feelings and anger hang out—just get them out of your system—and you'll solve your anger problems.*

Brenda, an attractive young secretary, is very aware of her hurt and angry feelings, but she would never dream of expressing them like Joe does. She tells me, "I can't get angry at anyone—if I could I wouldn't be here. I can't get angry because then no one would love me." She adds, "I can't even get mad at a guy who tries to seduce me."

Brenda typifies a host of patients I have known who wouldn't hurt anyone, who are never angry, and who seem to have an ideal temperament. Individuals like Brenda are friendly, well-liked, "nice" people. But they pay a tremendous price for their perpetual "niceness." After a few years physical and emotional illnesses often develop that affect their health, their relations with family members, and their job performance. Brenda is a victim of Misconception #4: *It won't cost me too much emotionally to be a nice person who never gets angry at anybody.*

Mary, a 42-year-old bank teller, sought my help for dizziness and stomach symptoms. Her internist had been unable to find an organic cause for her symptoms, which were so severe that they were interfering with her job. Upon questioning, Mary didn't seem to be harboring any bitterness or anger toward anybody she knew, including her husband of 20 years. But as therapy progressed it became apparent that she had buried a number of hurts over the years. At first she didn't see any correlation between these old hurts and her current symptoms.

Our next obstacle was to help her realize that a dedicated Christian could not only have such feelings but could resolve them in a constructive way. She was afraid that if she expressed her true feelings to her non-Christian husband, he would think less of her faith, or he might leave her, or he might even have a heart attack and die, leaving her to blame herself. She started gingerly applying the principles outlined in this book, and to her amazement, instead of the relationship with her husband being destroyed, a new-found love developed between them and her symptoms resolved themselves.

Mary illustrates Misconception #5: *If I express my hurts and anger to the person I'm angry at, our relationship will suffer.*

It is my opinion that at least 50 percent of all emotional, psychosomatic, and interpersonal problems (including familial and marital problems) are the result of poorly handled anger. What is more staggering is that a large percentage of these individuals don't even realize that they have an anger problem. Some of them may perhaps be aware that they are nursing a lot of old hurts, but many others are not aware of the role of feelings and anger in their lives.

Perhaps you've been saying to yourself as you've been reading about these patients, "I'm sure glad I don't have a problem with anger like they do." But before you put this book down, I ask you to consider the fact that it is precisely the person who thinks he never gets angry who often has the most serious problem with anger. He may sulk, whine, or stew; he may be cynical, envious, or catty; he may savor secret injustices, make caustic comments, or develop a martyr complex; but if you ask him if he has a problem with anger, he will smile innocently and say, "Why, no—I never get angry."

The problem is that this person doesn't see these things as symptomatic of an underlying problem with anger. Like many of us, he has a very simplistic notion of what anger is. Most of us think of a person who has a problem with anger as someone who yells at his kids and kicks his dog. But more often it is the person who suffers in stoic silence who has the problem. The people who bury anger or who express it in such camouflaged forms as bitterness, cynicism, or envy often fail to recognize the indicators of anger in their lives. They don't recognize as anger the little inner twinge when a friend makes an ever-so-carefully-phrased insult in the middle of a conversation. They don't recognize as anger the vague bitterness at their family for not appreciating all that they do for them.

Many people who are unable to recognize anger in their lives do sense that they have been hurt many times in the past, and that many of these hurts have not been resolved. If you are one of those individuals who usually senses hurts rather than actually feeling angry, perhaps it would be helpful for you to substitute the word "hurts" every time the word "anger" appears in this book to make it more applicable to you.

The root cause of many of these misconceptions about anger is a distrust and even a denial of our emotions. The fallacy of denying our emotions of hurt and anger can be illustrated by the following example.

My first car was plagued with a multitude of problems, and often the temperature needle would slowly rise higher and higher. My anxiety level would have a parallel response, and I'd nervously sweat out the miles to my destination or at least to the nearest gas station.

I could have saved myself a great deal of anguish by putting my hand over the gauge or even painting it black so I couldn't see the needle rise. It might have been more comfortable if I hadn't been warned of the impending danger. I might have saved myself a lot of alarming feelings. However, then the first indication of trouble might have been steam pouring out from under the hood, meaning that something was seriously wrong with the car.

Although painting over the temperature gauge may sound like a ridiculous thing to do, it is precisely what many people do with anger. They ignore it and even deny its very existence until it boils over, at which point they can't avoid it any longer. But by that time it may have caused incalculable damage to the person himself and to those around him.

I believe that one of the most important abilities and needs a person has is that of being aware of his own feelings. Many of us, particularly those of us with religious backgrounds, have been virtually robbed of the right to our feelings, especially feelings of anger. It's even comparable to a sort of psychological rape, in which a vital part of our humanity is violated, leaving us with irreparable emotional damage.

Our feelings are like a valuable guide, a sixth sense. They are an important clue to the unconscious and to issues of which we may not be totally aware. They are an invaluable monitor that alerts us to a side of an issue that is not being fully expressed at that time. However, feelings should never be regarded as mandates to action in themselves. They are incompletely formulated pieces of information—partial but vital bits of information that must be evaluated with knowledge, judgment, and understanding in order to give us a valid and complete picture of the situation.

Feelings are an indispensable part of our lives. They are vehicles to help us evaluate our actions. Losing the ability to be in touch with our feelings is tragic, certainly as grave in consequence as losing our sense of touch, taste, or smell. When we are in touch with our feelings we are best able to be in control of ourselves and to be responsive to those around us.

As a psychiatrist, I believe that anger that is inadequately dealt with is one of the most common problems today. Helping a patient recognize and deal constructively with his hurts and anger is one of the most important things that I can do professionally. I am convinced that if a person is able to handle the anger in his life maturely, he is probably mature in other respects of his life and is fairly free from emotional difficulty.

# Chapter

# Two

## *Mishandling Anger*

### Camouflaging Anger

Mr. Jones, a 58-year-old executive, sat in my office and told me that he wanted out of his marriage of 32 years. He felt he could cope better with divorce than with this marriage. He described himself as a person who wanted "peace at any price" after yielding for years to the pressures and demands of his wife. He was, as he put it, "always capitulating."

Mr. Jones said that he "faked the harmony" but always resented the deception. He concluded that it would take years to work out the problems in his marriage, and that he didn't have that much time left. For the first 20 years of his married life he hadn't been aware of what was going on. He became conscious of the unhealthy relationship 12 years ago, but hadn't altered his behavior. For the last six months he had been having physical symptoms, but they disappeared three weeks ago, when he told his wife he was leaving.

Mr. Jones illustrates one form that camouflaged anger can take—the don't-make-waves, *peace-at-any-price* individual. This individual will take the blame for anything, even things for which he is in no way responsible. He is self-effacing and never appears to be angry. But the peace is a sham. Often he has psychosomatic complaints which serve as a means of dissipating the anger. Frequently this kind of person is married to someone who expresses his or her feelings more overtly, thus tyrannizing the peace-at-any price individual. This person may think he is carrying out the Beatitudes because he is always turning the other cheek, but in reality it is a poor counterfeit. Sooner or later the results of this kind of pussyfooting will catch up with him.

Another way a person can camouflage his anger is by becoming a *stamp saver*. Sometimes this type of person is known as a martyr or a collector of injustices; I like to think of such people as stamp collectors. This person is the one who carefully saves up each little grievance, annoyance, or irritation. He tells himself that each grievance is not enough to deal with in itself. In fact, if asked, he would probably deny that there was anything bothering him at all. He may tell himself that the problem is so small that he shouldn't make an issue of it and that he should be able to forget it.

But in fact he doesn't forget. He pastes a stamp somewhere in his head. When the book gets full, he almost gleefully cashes it in. The last stamp may have been a very minor incident, but out comes pent-up rage that baffles the recipient and sometimes the stamp saver himself. This inappropriate outrage may then be justified by a detailed cataloging of all past offenses.

The third form that camouflaged anger can take is the *silent approach*. This person suddenly retreats into an icy silence when something is bothering him. If you ask if anything is wrong, he often flatly denies it, but he usually manages to let everyone know he's upset by making terse or grumpy remarks. Often the people around this silent person don't know what has upset him, and asking him doesn't help since he usually won't say anything until he is good and ready to do so.

Some years ago when I was practicing internal medicine, a colleague of mine referred a patient to me. As he was telling me about her physical complaints, he commented, "You know, she's *gooey sweet*—I'm sure she's covering up something, but I haven't yet figured out what it is." As I got to know this woman better, I became convinced that he was right. Her sweetness was saccharine and very tacky. There was something phony about it, something bitter and artificial. Often underneath this gooey-sweet facade is a great deal of anger.

Another camouflage is *the critic*. This individual is critical and sometimes sarcastic about everything. In comparison with the previous camouflages, this veneer tends to wear a bit thin. Often his criticisms are supported by seemingly well-founded intellectual or rational reasoning, but through it all something seems wrong, and one can sense an undertone of anger, hostility, and negativism.

The sixth form that camouflaged anger can take is that of the *passive-aggressive* person. This kind of person is characterized by aggressive behavior exhibited in passive ways such as pouting, stubbornness, and procrastination. He often takes the opposite point of view or opposes other people's actions. If you say you like jogging, for example, he will tell you how dangerous jogging can be. The next day if you say you don't like jogging, he'll tell you it's a great sport and everybody should take it up. If you say something is white, he'll call it black; if you say it's black, he'll say it's white. Such people are often late and keep others waiting for them. The passive-aggressive person tends to be a drag on others. Prolonged contact with this kind of person can be extremely frustrating.

Thus one can repress anger by camouflaging it in a variety of ways. The six ways mentioned above are not all-inclusive; there are as many ways of camouflaging anger as there are people to camouflage it. But it is interesting to note some of the major forms of emotional subterfuges we devise for ourselves— subterfuges that, sooner or later, must come out into the open.

### *Repressing Anger*

Many people who think that anger is wrong don't stop with just camouflaging it. They actually convince themselves that there is no anger in their lives. This denial of anger often occurs at an unconscious level, so that the people are unaware that they're doing this. They then try to convince others that they aren't angry. We're all familiar with the person who snaps, "No, I'm not angry!" when quite obviously he is. However, in some cases, the person who protests that he isn't angry is quite calm and collected and actually feels no anger. He may have repressed his anger to such a degree that he is completely numb to his feelings, while in reality a great deal of anger is buried underneath.

Anger, in my opinion, is like energy. It cannot be destroyed, but it can be stored or its form can be changed. When we bury the anger within us and repeatedly deny its existence, it accumulates in what I have chosen to call an *unresolved anger fund.* Dr. Rubin in *The Angry Book* refers to it as the slush fund (page 24). The more we push down anger, the more it accumulates. This accumulated anger will then express itself through any of the camouflages previously described, or it may convert its energy to more unrecognizable forms. It can lead to tremendous guilt, obesity, or insomnia. It can manifest itself in psychosomatic illnesses like backache, dermatological conditions, headaches, gastrointestinal symptoms, and ulcers. Other possible manifestations are sexual problems and fatigue.

People with these kinds of symptoms are too uncomfortable or too threatened to deal with the underlying feelings, so their unconscious mind tries to do them a favor by channeling the bottled-up feelings into the more-acceptable form of physical symptoms. The person has now compounded his problem: He is worried about a possible physical illness, and the real problem of anger is left unrecognized as the source of the problem.

Recent studies have shown that smokers have increased amounts of anger. Other studies indicate that hostility may be a precipitating factor in patients with high blood pressure. Hostility is also listed as one of the three major components of coronary-prone behavior, which tends to greatly increase one's chance of a heart attack. (See *Behavior Patterns, Stress and Coronary Disease*, by David Glass.) Patients with chronic pain syndromes also show increased levels of anger (*Audio-Digest Psychiatry*, Volume 6:24, 1977). The various types of patients, illnesses, and physical symptoms are probably legion.

In addition to the physical symptoms created by bottled-up anger, there are the more obvious emotional symptoms like depressions, neuroses, psychoses, and potentials for murder and suicide. This is not to imply that unresolved hurts and anger are the sole cause of all these symptoms, but they certainly comprise a major cause.

It is interesting to note that 60 percent of all homicides occur among family members, the home being the place where feelings are most apt to erupt. The most likely victim is usually one's spouse, lover, or friend, and the most likely place for the homicide to occur is in one's own home. Most murderers are, in fact, *not* persons with past criminal records.

Recently I heard a psychiatrist speak who had examined hundreds of prisoners charged or convicted of murder. He said that 70 to 80 percent of them hadn't wanted to hurt anyone, and they never seemed to get angry or to have any problem with anger. They were often law-abiding citizens who didn't even have a traffic ticket to their record. What happened? In my opinion, these are people who didn't know how to recognize and deal constructively with small amounts of anger, and so they allowed it to build in their unresolved anger fund. One slight provocation was then enough to fill the fund to the top and make them explode, usually taking out their violent feelings on someone they knew.

### The Overtly Angry Person

As noted in the two preceding sections, anger may be camouflaged or it may be denied so that the person is totally unaware of his own feelings.

The polar opposite of the person who denies anger is the person who is overtly angry. This person can be either chronically hostile or may just have occasional violent bursts of temper. Most talks, books, or sermons on anger are directed toward the person with this kind of anger. The church appropriately tells the chronically hostile person that his behavior needs changing. However, the sermon usually ends at that point, leaving the person to figure out on his own what is going on in his life and how to achieve that change in behavior. In addition, most of the people sitting in the pews handle their anger by repressing it, and thus the sermon doesn't help either group of individuals—either those who are overtly angry or those who repress their anger.

Joe, described in Chapter 1, comes to mind. Joe's concern was that people often tell him how hostile he is. He said that even strangers comment on his temper, one example being a waitress who had known him for only three minutes. He told me that he is sometimes aware that he is "slightly angry," but not to the extent or the degree that people tell him. Often he seems angry when he sees me for therapy, but if I ask him if he is, he denies it.

Since we have just discussed in such great detail the evils of camouflaging and denying anger, you might think that someone who expresses his anger as much as Joe does would be blissfully happy. But that isn't the case at all—Joe is chronically unhappy. He is frequently suicidal, and he has ostracized himself from almost all his friends and relatives.

During a recent appointment, Joe related how furious he was at his boss for criticizing his work one day. When I asked him how he had handled the situation, he said that he had felt the criticism was totally unjustified, but that he hadn't expressed his feelings to his boss. He kept them in, but remained very upset all day. However, when he went home that night, he blew up at his wife over a very inconsequential matter. The following day he had lunch with his boss and some employees. Some of the boss's comments sounded prejudiced to Joe, so he angrily criticized him in front of the other workers, calling him a bigot. This made Joe feel a little better because he had released his anger, but several days later in my office he was still licking his emotional wounds.

Let's take a look at the scorecard. I don't know if the boss's criticism was justified or not. If it was justified, Joe's problem was all the more complicated. But let's assume that the boss was wrong. The initial hurt and anger from the original insult had not been dealt with in any constructive way, either by talking it over with the boss or by reconciling it within himself. Then he had created problems at home by taking out his frustrations on his family. In addition, criticizing his boss at lunch only further complicated the situation. None of his actions led to any resolution of the initial problem. In fact, they only intensified his problems, and a few weeks later Joe impetuously quit his job because he couldn't handle the pressures there any longer. This placed further strain on his horrible financial situation and led him very close to committing suicide. Thus, expressing his anger was not the answer. His need was to handle his anger in a constructive way.

# Chapter

# Three

## *Biblical Principles*

### The Contradiction

By this time I'm sure many of you are saying, "Wait a minute—are you saying anger is *right?* How do you explain away the verses in the Bible that say anger is a sin?"

Some verses do say that anger is wrong. Ephesians 4:31 says, "Let all . . . anger . . . be put away." Psalm 37:8 says, "Cease from anger," and the Sermon on the Mount teaches, "If you are only *angry,* even in your own home, you are in danger of judgment" (Matthew 5:22 TLB).

On the other hand, some parts of the Bible seem to condone anger. Perhaps the most striking verses to this effect are Psalm 4:4 and Ephesians 4:26. Psalm 4:4 reads, "Be angry, but sin not" (RSV). The same thought is repeated in Ephesians 4:26: "Be angry, and yet do not sin." One commentator writes, "The words 'be ye angry' are a present imperative in the Greek text, commanding a continuous action" (*Wuest's Word Studies from the Greek New Testament for the English Reader*, page 114). Thus it can almost be construed as a command to be angry under certain conditions.

A careful study of the Bible reveals that most of the important characters in it got angry, contrary to the stereotypes we have of them today. Moses was a patriarch who without question was blessed of God. However, he sometimes became extremely angry. For example, when Moses returned from receiving the Ten Commandments and the Law from God on Mount Sinai, he discovered that in his absence the Israelites had started worshiping idols. He became so enraged that he smashed the stone tablets on which the Law was written (Exodus 32:19).

David was described as a man after God's own heart (Acts 13:22), yet he became angry at God when a man was killed trying to protect the ark of God (2 Samuel 6:6-8).

We could cite dozens of verses in which men of God got angry. However, we still might not be able to conclude anything, because it could be argued that they were sinning in each case. For example, one could argue that while Moses should indeed have reprimanded the Israelites, he should not have let himself get so carried away that he smashed the sacred Law of God. One could also argue that David should certainly not have shaken his fist at the heavens and argued with God (2 Samuel 6:8).

Nevertheless, there are two Personages in the Bible whom we cannot accuse of sinning when they got angry.

Do you know who in the Bible got angry the most often? Not the Pharisees, nor the Philistines, nor any other assorted heathen. It was God Himself—God, who is without sin. The Hebrew word for anger appears approximately 455 times in the Old Testament, and of these, 375 times it is referring to the anger of God.

Jesus also became quite angry at times, contrary to the image we have of Him as a bland, quiet soul. He got upset when He saw the hardened, callous hearts of the people as He was about to heal the man with a paralyzed hand (Mark 3:1-5). In Mark 11:15-17 we find Him driving out the parasitic money changers in the temple with a whip, shouting after them, "Is it not written, My house shall be called a house of prayer for all nations? But you have made it a robbers' den." In Matthew 23 He lashes out at the smug, hypocritical Pharisees, calling them "whitewashed tombs . . . full of dead men's bones!"

Thus some verses indicate that we shouldn't be angry, while others almost tell us that if we are to follow Christ's and God's examples, there are times when we should be angry. How can we reconcile this apparent contradiction? How can we reconcile one verse in which God Himself is angry with another verse in which God commands us not to be angry?

### Biblical Analysis

Studying the meanings of the various words for anger in the original languages in which the Bible was written might shed considerable light upon this matter. It might turn out that there are different words for anger with different connotations or shades of meaning. For example, there could be one word for anger which denotes God's justified anger, meaning a sort of detached, righteous indignation, while a different word could be used for Saul's unjustified anger when he tried to kill David, meaning a malicious, vindictive rage (1 Samuel 19:10).

The Hebrew word most frequently translated "anger" comes from the word *aph.* This word appears several hundred times in the Hebrew Old Testament. It is usually used to describe God's obviously appropriate anger, such as appears in Numbers 11:1: "Now the people became like those who complain of adversity in the hearing of the Lord; and when the Lord heard it, His anger was kindled, and the fire of the Lord burned among them and consumed some of . . . the camp." This same word *aph* describes Moses' strong but questionable emotions when he smashed the stone tablets against the mountain.

Not only is this word used to describe God's appropriate anger and Moses' questionable anger, but it is also the word used to denote clearly inappropriate anger, as in the case of Balaam (Numbers 22:27). Psalm 37:8 also uses this word: "Cease from anger, and forsake wrath; fret not yourself in any way to do evil" (KJV). Thus exactly the same word is used to describe appropriate, questionable, and inappropriate anger.

When we turn to the New Testament, one of the more common words translated "anger" is *orge*. This Greek word originally referred to any natural impulse, desire, or disposition. Later it came to signify anger. It was thought of as an internal motion, like the juices in plants or fruit, and meant the natural disposition, temper, character, or impulse of a thing. Just as in the Old Testament, this word is sometimes used to describe appropriate anger, such as God's or

Christ's (Hebrews 3:11; Romans 9:22; Mark 3:5). Yet it is the same word that is translated "anger" in Ephesians 4:31: "Let all bitterness and wrath and anger and clamor and slander be put away from you, along with all malice." (See also Colossians 3:8.) The same word is used in James 1:19: "Let everyone be quick to hear, slow to speak, and slow to *anger*." Thus this word is also used to describe appropriate and inappropriate anger.

Another Greek word, *orgizo,* means "to be angry." It is the word used in Matthew 5:22: "But I say unto you, whosoever is angry with his brother without a cause shall be in danger of judgment" (KJV). This is an extremely strong injunction against this kind of anger. Yet it is exactly the same word that is used in Ephesians 4:26: "Be angry, and yet do not sin."

### *The Logical Conclusion*

I believe that the logical conclusion we can draw is that each of the words translated "anger" is used in neutral, negative, or positive ways, and that we must look at the context of each verse to see whether the anger is justified or not.

Likewise, in our own lives we must look at the context of each situation to judge whether our anger is justified or not. Anger is *in and of itself* neutral; it is neither right nor wrong, appropriate nor inappropriate, holy nor sinful. Nor has it anything to do with how intense the anger is. In some cases we may actually be sinning by only being mildly irritated when it may be God's will for us to be very angry.

*It is what the anger is based on and how the anger is expressed* that determines whether it is right or wrong. This parallels perfectly the usual psychological view of anger, which says that anger is an emotion that is in itself neutral but which may have an inappropriate or an appropriate basis, and that anger may be used destructively or constructively.

### Biblical Principles About Anger

The scriptures offer many guidelines for handling anger properly. First of all, it should be understood that feelings of anger, as well as feelings of all kinds, are God-given gifts. According to Genesis 1:26,27, God in His wisdom created us in His own image, and it is my belief that one of the things He created us with was the ability to get angry. Feelings can be used to serve us and to serve God well. To deny them is to deny a part of the person God created us to be.

James reminds his readers in James 5:17 that godly men of old, like Elijah, were human beings with feelings like ours, something we are prone to forget. Anger can be likened to power, sex, or fire: They are things that are neither right nor wrong in themselves, but rather in how they are used. Christians today are trying to make anger wrong, just like earlier generations tried to make virtually all sex wrong, with equally disastrous results.

I believe that the Scriptures teach that if we deny our anger we are in fact sinning. Whether the basis for the anger is right or wrong is immaterial at this point. If anger exists and you deny its presence to yourself or others, you are living a lie. That is sin. Even if you know that in a particular situation it is wrong for you to be angry, to lie about it is to add one sin upon another. In addition, denying our anger vastly complicates working out the problem with our fellow human beings. In Ephesians 4:25 we read, "Therefore, laying aside falsehood, speak truth, each one of you, with his neighbor, for we are members of one another."

A crucial principle is that a person should listen to his feelings but never be controlled by them. James 1:19 says, "Let everyone be quick to hear, slow to speak, and slow to anger." We are told in Proverbs 16:32, "He who is slow to anger is better than the mighty, and he who rules his spirit than he who captures a city." Proverbs 19:11 adds, "A man's discretion makes him slow to anger." Thus we should be sensitive to our feelings, but never controlled by them or compelled to act on the basis of our feelings alone.

Closely related to this is not being hasty in dealing with our anger. Ecclesiastes 7:9 says, "Be not hasty in thy spirit to be angry" (KJV). James 1:19 tells us that we should be slow to take offense and to get angry. Proverbs 25:8 says, "Do not go out hastily to argue your case." (See also Proverbs 15:18; Titus 1:7; Psalm 103:8; 145:8; Nehemiah 9:17.)

Just as we should not be in a hurry to deal with anger, we must also not go to the opposite extreme and delay longer than is necessary. This is an extremely important point. If you are in a situation with another person in which you react with feelings of hurt or anger, and you know that you need to talk to that individual about it, it is far preferable to take the appropriate action in a matter of seconds or minutes (or at the most a few hours after the incident) than to wait days, weeks, months, or even years before constructively handling the situation. The emotional weight which untold millions of people carry simply because they have procrastinated at this point would stagger your mind.

Ephesians 4:26 is very applicable to this problem—"Be angry, and yet do not sin; do not let the sun go down on your anger." Not letting the sun go down on your anger seems to have three possible interpretations. First of all, the usual interpretation is that it is referring to *time*—that is, that we should resolve or deal with the anger the same day or at least in very close proximity to the event which caused the anger.

According to Vine's *Expository Dictionary of New Testament Words* (Volume III, p. 93), the word *helios,* which is translated "the sun," can also mean "the natural benefits of light and heat . . . and judgment." Thus it seems that an alternate rendering might be, "Don't wait so long in dealing with the anger that the intensity of the *feeling* decreases and sets within you before you take appropriate action." I believe it can be useful to deal with the issue while you still feel angry, if certain stipulations are met which will be discussed in detail later.

Several verses in the Bible refer to the day as the time of *opportunity* (John 9:4). Thus a third possible interpretation is to deal with our feelings while there is still an opportunity.

In summary, a possible interpretation of Ephesians 4:26 might read like this: "It's appropriate and necessary to be angry, but be very careful that you don't sin in the process. Dissipate the anger constructively before the heat of the emotion is lost, too much time passes, and the best opportunity is gone."

Another principle taught in the Scriptures is that when you are angry you are much more vulnerable to sin. Note the sequence of Ephesians 4:26 and 4:27: "Be angry, and yet do not sin; do not let the sun go down on your anger, *and do not give the devil an opportunity*." An example of this is illustrated in Numbers 20:7-11. Moses was angry at the Israelites, and God gave him instructions on how to deal with the problem. Moses disobeyed the instructions, probably because he neglected to hear what God was telling him because he was so angry. Similarly, our own anger can drown out what God is telling us and can "give the devil an opportunity." Proverbs 29:22 warns, "An angry man stirs up strife, and a hot-tempered man abounds in transgression." Proverbs 14:29 adds, "A wise man controls his temper. He knows that anger causes mistakes" (TLB).

Another version of Ephesians 4:26 focuses on the danger of nursing our anger and letting it turn into bitterness and resentment: "If you are angry, do not let anger lead you into sin; do not let sunset find you still nursing it; leave no loop-hole for the devil" (NEB). The Scriptures teach that the persistent anger which makes us bitter and resentful is probably always sin. Hebrews 12:15 says, "See to it . . . that no root of bitterness springing up causes trouble, and by it many be defiled."

We mechanically repeat the part of the Lord's Prayer that says, ''Forgive us our debts, as we forgive our debtors,'' but very few of us stop to consider the consequences of what we are saying. The Amplified Bible's interpretation of the verse immediately following the Lord's Prayer says that if we do not give up our resentment, God will not forgive our sins (Matthew 6:15). Thus, clinging stubbornly to resentment is very destructive to the person himself, because it blocks God's forgiveness. This scriptural principle helps explain the relationship between guilt and unresolved anger. This topic will be discussed in greater detail later in this book.

The Scriptures also teach that vindictive, malicious anger is wrong. Almost every time the phrase ''Cease from anger'' is found in the Bible, it is in the context of wrath or vindictiveness. For example, Psalm 37:8 says, ''Cease from anger, and forsake wrath.'' Romans 12:18-21 says, ''If possible, so far as it depends on you, be at peace with all men. Never take your own revenge, beloved, but leave room for the wrath of God, for it is written, 'Vengeance is Mine, I will repay, says the Lord.' But if your enemy is hungry, feed him, and if he is thirsty, give him a drink; for in so doing you will heap burning coals upon his head. Do not be overcome by evil, but overcome evil with good.''

As one might suspect, there are times when anger is wrong because it is unjustly or inappropriately based. Second Chronicles 16:7-10 tells us that Asa put his trust in the king of Syria instead of in God. A prophet told him that his country would have wars because of his sin. Asa became angry, put the prophet in jail, and oppressed all the people. He became angry because he didn't like what he heard even though it was the truth, and so he took out his anger on others.

In 1 Kings 20 and 21, King Ahab became angry and resentful because he was told the consequences of his own sin and because he didn't get his own way. Obviously, both of these men's anger was far from righteous. If we have expectations that are inappropriate or sinful, and we become angry because we don't get our way, we are sinning in our anger.

The final principle—and perhaps the most startling one—is that in some cases anger may be righteous and its absence may displease God. In other words, we may be sinning by not getting angry. First Samuel 11:6 reads, ''Then the Spirit of God came upon Saul mightily when he heard these words, and he became very angry.'' The passage goes on to indicate that Saul's anger and the resulting action he took were appropriate and righteous. In Nehemiah 5:6-9, a prophet, speaking as God's messenger, became angry at the people as he reprimanded them for their sin. God even commanded Moses to be angry, in Numbers 25:16,17: "The Lord spoke to Moses, saying, 'Be hostile to the Midianites and strike them.'"

Have you ever considered the possibility that Christ might have been sinning if he hadn't gotten angry at the moneychangers in the temple? There are other examples in the Scriptures of people who probably were sinning because they didn't get angry enough to do anything. For example, when God warned Eli because he didn't rebuke his sons for their sinning, Eli took God's warning very passively. Even when God told Eli that He would kill Eli's entire household, including Eli, all he said was, "Let Him do what seems good." This is in distinct contrast to what most prophets did when they heard God's judgment—they got upset enough to forcefully warn the people to turn from their wicked ways, often with the result that God retracted the punishment.

While Moses was receiving the Ten Commandments from God on Mount Sinai, Aaron was completely passive when the Israelites wanted him to make an idol for them to worship. Exodus 32:25 says, "The people were out of control, for Aaron had let them get out of control." Aaron would have

been better off if he had had some of Moses'
tablet-smashing anger!

The church leaders at Corinth probably
would not have received such a strong
rebuke from Paul if they had stirred up
enough anger to take appropriate action
against the incestuous church member (see 1
Corinthians 5). Considering these examples,
another rendering of "Be angry but do not
sin" might be "Be appropriately angry and
thereby do not sin." In my opinion, many
people don't get angry when they should and
therefore do not mobilize the energy necessary to deal with some crucially important
issues of life.

# Chapter

# Four

## *How Do You Handle Your Anger?*

Anger is generally defined as a strong feeling of hostility or indignation. It is a state of emotional excitement induced by intense displeasure as a result of a real or imagined threat, insult, put-down, frustration, or injustice to yourself or to others who are important to you. If the displeasure is very great and is processed through the conscious portion of the mind, it activates the "fight-or-flight" mechanism in the body, which prepares it for battle or escape. This mechanism releases adrenalin, which in turn increases the blood pressure, pulse, and respiratory rate. One may perspire or feel edgy as a result of the surge of energy which has literally infused the entire body. These intense *feelings* of displeasures are what most people associate with being angry.

However, it is my opinion that this is an incomplete view of anger. If over a period of years an individual repeatedly rejects these *feelings* of displeasure, the unconscious mind will take control, eliminating the *feeling* portion of the process. The person may then *feel* nothing. However, the cost will be very great because the emotionally charged displeasure will then be buried in the unconscious, only to seek expression later in one or more of the forms or camouflages described earlier. Thus a seemingly calm and controlled person may in fact have a more serious problem with anger than the person who stomps around the house yelling at people.

Most individuals use varying degrees of their conscious and unconscious minds to process their feelings of displeasure, and anger can be manifested in many different forms. It can *feel* like "nothing," numbness, hurt, disappointment, frustration, irritation, annoyance, or rage, to name a few possibilities.

Anger may be defined as an automatic reaction to any real or imagined insult, frustration, or injustice, producing emotional agitation, which the person may or may not be aware of, but which will seek expression in some sort of aggressive, defensive, or destructive manner to oneself or others.

### Obvious and Hidden Anger

Anger may be camouflaged, so that others are unaware of the person's anger, or it may be denied, so that the person himself is unaware of his feelings. Anger can take a number of forms, with each form varying as to how visible this anger is to the person himself and to those around him.

With the overtly angry person, everyone is quite aware of the fact that the person is very angry—both the person himself and those around him. We may say that this person's feelings are *known*. With the person who has camouflaged his anger fairly well, the world at large may not be aware of his feelings because they are *hidden;* that is, they are hidden from others, but the person himself may be aware of them. Thirdly, the world at large may be aware of the person's anger, but the person himself is *blind* to it. Last of all, and most serious of all, is the person whose anger has been so denied and repressed that neither the person himself nor the world around him is aware that it is buried within him. There may be some physical or emotional symptoms, but the angry feelings causing them are *unknown,* locked up in the person's unconscious for the time being.

These various situations can be illustrated by a large square divided into four equal squares (see Illustration 1), a diagram which has been adapted from the Johari Window, first described by Luft and Ingham in 1955.

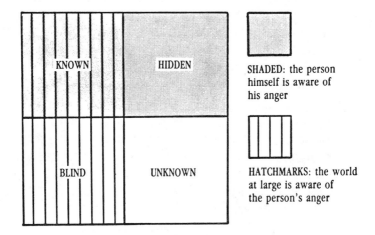

SHADED: the person himself is aware of his anger

HATCHMARKS: the world at large is aware of the person's anger

**Illustration 1**
**Visibility of Anger**

The upper two squares with shading represent that the person himself is aware of his anger. The two squares on the left side with hatchmarks represent that the world at large is aware of the person's anger.

These then break down into four categories or four squares. In the square in the upper left-hand corner, both the person himself and the world at large are aware of the person's anger, as indicated by the combined hatchmarks and shading. This person's feelings are *known*.

In the square in the lower right-hand corner, neither the person himself nor the world at large are aware of the person's anger, as indicated by the lack of hatchmarks and shading. This persons' feelings are *unknown*.

In the square in the upper right-hand corner, the person himself is aware of the anger, but the world isn't, as indicated by the shading. This person's anger is *hidden*.

In the square in the lower left-hand corner, the person himself is unaware of his anger, but the world at large is aware of it, as indicated by the hatchmarks. This person is *blind* to his own anger.

The person whose anger is *known* is seen by the world as an angry, hostile person, and the person himself feels very angry. He may also feel abused and misunderstood. Though this person is aware of a great deal of hostility in his life, there also may be areas where he is not aware of his anger.

The square labeled HIDDEN represents the individual whose anger is basically concealed from the world around him, although the person himself is aware that the anger is there. He is probably expending a great deal of energy trying to camouflage it by being gooey-sweet or overly critical, or by using any of the other subterfuges previously discussed. He may have other problems which people see, although they are not aware that anger is the root cause of these problems.

In the case of the person who is *blind* to his own anger, the world at large is aware that this person is angry, upset, or difficult to get along with, but the person himself is unaware that anger is his basic problem. He may be unhappy, discontented, or tired, but he is unaware of the fact that he has failed to deal with anger in his life.

Finally, we have the person whose anger is *unknown* to himself or to those around him. It has been repressed to the point that the nature of the problem is lost and distorted. This individual often has difficulty in being in touch with any of his feelings, to such a degree that he is totally numb. He may have numerous psychosomatic problems; he may be confused or psychotic. He may appear to be cold and aloof, but neither he nor the world around him is aware of the important role of anger in the development of his problems.

This is obviously oversimplified—people cannot be categorized so neatly into one of four little squares—but it does help illustrate how feelings can be present in our lives, yet still be unknown to ourselves or to those around us. There are several important points that we can learn from this illustration.

One point is that other people may be aware of a person's anger while the person himself may not be. Thus it is often crucial that the person remain open to the input of others in understanding oneself.

Secondly, both the person himself and others may be totally unaware that anger is the problem, and thus one can spend untold hours and dollars trying to find other causes for the physical and emotional symptoms. If we fail to recognize the fact that anger can be the cause of a host of seemingly unrelated physical and emotional problems, we won't get very far when we try to treat the problem.

Finally, we need to be fully aware of what a shadowy, slippery thing anger is. We tend to think of anger in very simplistic terms—if someone yells and throws coffee cups, we aptly conclude that he is an angry person. But as we have seen, anger can take a variety of forms and can be concealed in many ways. I would encourage you to think about where you fit into this diagram, and seriously consider whether you are hiding anything from those around you, or even from yourself.

### Levels of Maturity in Handling Anger

For years I have heard suggestions like "Slam the door, it will do you good" as a way for people to deal with their anger. Many times I have wrestled with these ideas. Do I agree with this? Is it good to slam a door? Is that the best way to handle anger? Is it better than the other ways people use? I came to the conclusion that slamming a door may be a positive step for someone who is not in touch with his anger or who always buries it. On the other hand, some people who slam doors also break furniture. For them, slamming doors won't be beneficial unless it is a less destructive act than they might otherwise have performed. On the other hand, a more mature individual may actually be regressing if he slams a door.

The thing to realize is that we don't either handle anger constructively or not handle it constructively, with no stages in-between. Rather, there are various levels of maturity in which we can deal with our anger. Thus the method of treatment varies somewhat according to how maturely the person handles his anger, just as a medical prescription varies according to how physically sick a patient is. We must resist the temptation to give blanket solutions to the anger problem. We cannot tell everybody that the way to cure their anger problem is to slam the door. For some people this would do a world of good, but for those who have already broken every door and window in the house, this would obviously not be advisable.

To help clarify the different levels of maturity and also to help you pinpoint where you might be in the total spectrum of how to handle anger, I have made the following diagram (see Illustration 2).

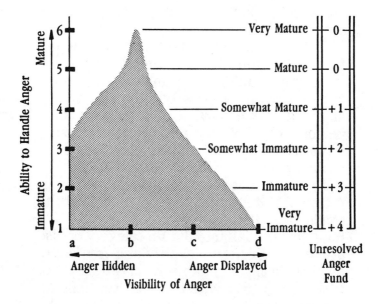

**Illustration 2**
**Visibility and Maturity of Handling Anger**

The vertical axis represents one's maturity in handling anger—the higher the level on the page, the more mature the person is. A maturity level of 1 indicates a very immature person, while a maturity level of 6 indicates a very mature person.

The horizontal axis represents the visibility of the anger. The farther to the right of the graph, the more displayed the person's anger is. A person whose anger is well-hidden would be at "a" while a person whose anger is typically displayed would be at "d".

The shaded area represents the actual feasible positions. For example, the point "6-d" represents a very mature person (6) and a person who is overtly chronically angry (d). Obviously, it is impossible for a person to be both very mature and overtly, typically angry, so "6-d" is not part of the shaded area.

If we consider the *very immature* person in category 1, it is apparent from looking at the shaded area that he may at one extreme hide his anger and fall into the 1-a category or else at the other extreme overtly and frequently display his anger and thus be in category 1-d. It doesn't matter where this person falls on the line between 1-a and 1-d; there is still the same degree of immaturity. The only difference is how apparent it is to those observing this individual. The 1-d person will appear to be angry, hostile, and even abusive—the stereotypical "immature" person. On the other hand, the 1-a person may appear on the surface to handle his anger very maturely because he is very calm and unemotional in time of stress. But in reality he is as immature as the hostile 1-d person.

Moving to the top of the diagram, we find the person who is *very mature* in handling anger. The next question is whether we can consider someone to be very mature who typically hides his anger. My conclusion is that this is virtually impossible; thus no 6-a is shown. Likewise, a person cannot be chronically angry and yet be very mature in the way he handles anger, so no 6-c or 6-d is shown.

How visible is the very mature person's anger? Is he always calm, cool, and collected—the stereotypical "always-nice" person? It is my opinion that if a person is always "nice" in every setting, he will have to bury some anger, because conflict is occasionally inevitable. Also, if he takes a stand on righteous principles (discussed later in this book) he will face additional conflicts. Thus the very mature individual will occasionally have to display anger; therefore I have placed him at 6-b.

Only as one moves down the graph to more immature ways of handling anger do people tend to chronically hide their anger or express it more overtly.

The Unresolved Anger Fund, on the right-hand side of Illustration 2, also fits well into this scheme. The very mature person has a zero balance in his fund, whereas the very immature person has a large amount, indicated by a +4.

Let's examine each of these categories more carefully and describe the characteristics of people in the various levels of maturity.

### *Very Mature (Category 6)*

This is the most mature way an individual can handle anger. This person is fully aware of the environment around him and his own feelings, including feelings of hurt and anger. He is able to accurately determine the reasons for his feelings. He is aware of the primary feelings causing anger as well as the secondary feelings of anger. He has no unresolved anger in his potential unresolved anger fund.

The very mature person has full control of his actions. His response is by choice rather than by reaction. He may choose any of the constructive means to handle anger that will be discussed later, but two in particular stand out. This person is able to *act out of principle,* meaning that when other people's lives are at stake and injustices are done, this person gets angry, and his anger leads to positive action. An example of this is when Christ threw out the money changers in the temple (John 2). Paul had the same kind of righteous displeasure when he contended with Peter over legalism.

The second major way that this person constructively deals with his anger is to *suppress* his feelings and dissipate them without either harming the people around him or holding the anger inside so that it is destructive to himself. An example of this is how Christ handled the people who laughed at him for saying Jarius' daughter was dead (Matthew 9). He disagreed with the crowd, went in to see the girl, and raised her from the dead. Notice that Jesus didn't need to take the girl before the crowd and say, "I told you so," as you and I might have done. The person with Christlike maturity doesn't need to defend himself. The only person who has ever achieved this degree of maturity in handling his anger is Christ himself.

### *Mature (Category 5)*

The mature person is always aware of his feelings and is able to accurately determine their cause. He is aware of his anger as well as of the primary feelings causing it. He constructively dissipates his negative feelings in a way that harms others the least. He may

not always be able to act out of pure principles or always be able to suppress his personal feelings, but when he expresses them,
they are in fairly innocuous ways. He has no
significant anger in his unresolved anger
fund. This is probably the most mature person you will ever meet. He is very kind, con-
siderate, and aware of his own and others'
feelings. Many annoyances that bother other
people really won't bother this person.
When something really does bother him, this
person can be counted on to confront the
situation squarely. He will never avoid a
problem merely because it is uncomfortable
to deal with.

### *Somewhat Mature (Category 4)*

This individual is aware of his feelings of
anger and often is aware of his primary feelings and their cause. He attempts to deal
fairly quickly with the problem, but
occasionally may react too quickly or slowly.
He may not always be as kind as possible to
the person he is interacting with, but his
basic desire is to resolve the problem. As indicated on the diagram, this person may tend
to hide his feelings more and thus may move
toward the category 4-a, or he may be more
overt and thus fall into the category of 4-c.
This person may have a small amount of
anger in his unresolved anger fund.

Probably most of the more-mature people you know fall into this category. They are quite mature individuals but may occasionally bury some feelings that should be dealt with or slightly blow it when expressing feelings of hurt or anger. Family members may occasionally hear this person yell. But he will quickly try to remedy the situation and will be willing to apologize when appropriate.

### Somewhat Immature (Category 3)

As we move further down the graph toward the somewhat immature person, we find that this person is usually aware of his negative feelings, but only occasionally knows the specific causes of them. He occasionally makes attempts to deal with feelings constructively, but at other times handles them destructively. This person never seriously injures anyone, but he may cause a fair amount of emotional hurt to those around him. He has collected a moderate amount of anger in his unresolved anger fund. There may be significant neurotic symptoms, psychosomatic complaints, marital problems, or other difficulties.

The person who tends to bury anger falls into the 3-a category. He may sulk, be passive-aggressive, or use other methods, but externally he looks fairly well-adjusted to all but those who are extremely close to him. It's likely that you know many people in this category, though they may hide the fact from you. The person who is more overtly angry is in category 3-c. This person loses his temper, slams doors, and may even break things in his attempts to give vent to his anger. Those who know him consider him to be somewhat hostile or to have a bad temper.

It is important to note that a younger person can be handling anger immaturely but may not yet exhibit any of the physical or psychological symptoms simply because he or she is so young. As you will see in the next chapter, the toll on us and our bodies accumulates as the years pass if we remain in one of the more-immature categories of handling our anger. So if you don't have any of the symptoms listed for people who handle anger immaturely, don't take it as conclusive proof that all is well.

### Immature (Category 2)

The immature person handles anger more poorly than people in the above categories. He may hide his anger and fall into category 2-a. This person often denies the existence of any anger in his life. When he is aware of any anger, he still often handles it destructively. He has a large unresolved anger fund, which persists in making him uncomfortable and unhappy. He may have a number of physical symptoms. Often there is a lot of guilt and depression in his life, or he may be numb to his feelings. Suicidal thoughts may start to emerge. Still, this immature person may be able to hide his problems from all but those who are very close to him.

In contrast, 2-c is as immature as 2-a, but those around him know that he is angry. He typically overreacts to small irritants and may not be aware of why he is reacting the way he is. Even when he is aware of what is making him angry, he usually handles his anger destructively. He often makes other people unhappy and may even hurt them physically. Emotional scars are inevitable, and are particularly apparent to his spouse and children.

Individuals in this category rarely sit down and honestly share their feelings with others. Those who hide their anger try to avoid conflict issues, only to have the effects emerge later in indirect ways. The overtly angry person is prone to launch an angry counterattack, often confusing the issue and leaving others hurt.

### Very Immature (Category 1)

The very immature person chronically hides his anger and is in category 1-a. He may be totally unaware that anger is a problem for him, and so he typically handles it destructively. Generally he doesn't want to hurt anyone, but his problem is so great that it is virtually impossible for him to avoid creating a lot of problems for others as well as for himself. If he is not extremely depressed, he is then emotionally numb. Inevitably there are a lot of physically distressing symptoms, if not a neurosis or even a psychosis. This person has a gigantic unresolved anger fund. He can no longer hide his dilemma from the outside world; they know he is in trouble and that without a drastic change the anger may lead to depression and hopelessness of such magnitude that it may result in suicide. Occasionally this person becomes so angry that he bursts like a boiling teapot, perhaps even hurting others.

The person who is very immature in handling anger and who displays it would fall into the category of 1-c or 1-d. This individual is obviously extremely hostile and physically abusive to those who get in his way. He causes others much unhappiness and is a very unhappy person himself. He may use alcohol and have trouble with the law. He may feel guilty and depressed, feelings that may lead to homicide or suicide.

### Summary

This graph, with all its various vertical and horizontal axes, from varying degrees of maturity in handling anger to varied degrees of visibility of anger, is not meant to be merely an intellectually satisfying way of measuring the anger situation. Rather, it has been devised with the purpose of helping *you* pinpoint just how maturely you handle anger.

I would encourage you to take a moment to consider what category you fit into. Think of various conflict situations you have experienced in the past—a snub from a friend, an irritation at the office, a terse conversation at home—and analyze the maturity of your responses. Consider things like whether you use any camouflages, whether you try to avoid conflicts, whether you snap at trivial details, whether your anger is visible to to those who know you, and whether you take out your frustrations on others.

With mutual consent, you may want to consider how those who are close to you handle their anger (whether husband, wife, parents, or roommates), and then consider how the combination of the way each of you handles anger affects the relationship. But don't get so sidetracked with the relatively joyous task of analyzing other people's flaws that you forget to consider whether you might have one or two of your own.

# Chapter

# Five

## *Preparing to Handle Anger*

### Conflict Is Normal and Inevitable

Two important things to grasp before trying to deal with anger are that conflict is both normal and inevitable. Most of us agree intellectually that being irritated or upset is a normal part of everyday existence, but emotionally we often don't really accept this. We feel vaguely guilty for getting mad at someone; we try not to think about it, and we wish the problem would just go away so we could get back to everyday life. But conflict *is* a part of life. Yet we tend to look upon it as an abnormal state, as a sign of deficiency.

We need to realize that having angry feelings toward a loved one doesn't mean that we don't love him. Many people feel secretly guilty every time they get angry at someone because they think that if they loved that person enough, they wouldn't get mad at him. It's true that newlyweds in a state of matrimonial bliss can often ignore little things that normally would irritate them. But this should be regarded as an emotional phase—certainly a desirable one, but an unrealistic standard for everyday living.

Having perfect Christlike love for someone doesn't mean that his snoring doesn't bother you. Again, let us look to Christ for our example. Undoubtedly He had perfect Christlike love for people, but as we have already seen, that didn't mean He never got angry at them.

It is simply a fact of life that the people who are the closest to you are the people with whom you are most likely to get angry. These are the people with whom you have the most interchange and about whom you have the highest expectations, and as a result they are the people with whom you have the greatest possibility of being angry. Expect that you are going to get angry at the people who are close to you. Expect it because it is, in fact, normal; it is a part of life, a part of the dynamics of two people living close to each other.

In addition to accepting the fact that anger is normal, we need to accept the fact that it is inevitable. Just yesterday I saw a 31-year-old man who had buried his hurts and anger for many years, and in the last two years has had physical symptoms. Only in the last couple of months has he been aware of, or at least willing to admit, the emotional basis.

Yesterday he told me, "I just want it [the problem] to go away. I don't want any hassles." For 20 minutes we talked about his suicidal wishes. He just wanted to die or to get into a bad car accident, but, not wanting to hurt others, he rejected these ideas. At the end of the appointment he told me that he didn't want to talk about his problems anymore—even that was too much of a hassle. So he left, not planning to see me anymore, refusing any referrals or any of the other options offered to him. My heart was very heavy because I knew he was again taking the easy way out, with the strong possibility of suicide as a consequence.

Part of this man's problem was that he was unwilling to accept the inevitability of conflict in his life. He just wanted the problem to go away. He didn't want any hassles. Many of us, whether we realize it or not, have this same attitude to various degrees. Many people who come to see me professionally dislike emotional conflict intensely and will go to great lengths to avoid it. They may remark, "I don't like conflict," or "I hate to argue," or "I can't stand to be around people when they are angry at each other." Though I have never had a person actually come out and tell me he wants a conflict-free environment, this is what people are implying.

The only way that such psychological bliss might be achieved would be by going to a deserted island. On the island, one would have to be careful not to communicate with anyone, either by telephone or by letter. No one would be allowed to come ashore because then some conflict would eventually develop. Even then, it is doubtful whether one would be totally free of conflict, because there would probably be a degree of internal stress, to say nothing about insects, shark-infested waters, and adverse weather.

But as we all know, no man is an island. Rather, we are inextricably woven to each other by complicated interpersonal relationships. The following illustrations show the various ways that people handle the conflicts that inevitably arise in each of these relationships.

Illustration 3-a shows two people with the normal conflicts of an interpersonal relationship. **(See next page)**

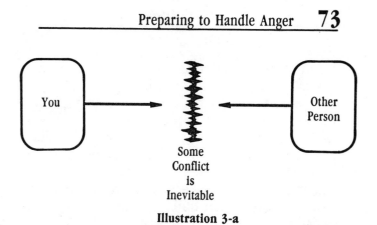

**Illustration 3-a**

Illustration 3-b represents the individual who would like no conflict at all. He might even marry someone who feels the same as he. However, in my experience with couples such as this, where each is ultrasensitive to conflict and shuns it at all costs, I have observed that feelings are not shared adequately and new conflicts arise within the people themselves. In addition, there is

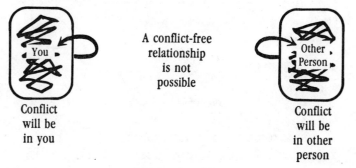

**Illustration 3-b**

bound to be conflict as the people interact with the world outside the home.

More common than the situation in which two people avoid conflict equally is the situation in which only one person avoids it. This person will yield to the other, always giving in, squelching his own feelings and legitimate needs in the process. This can go on for a while, but eventually these legitimate needs will cry out for expression. In addition, the friend or spouse often tends to be more forthright in expressing his or her wishes, which only pushes the other person's conflict further within. Many times the forthright person isn't even aware that he is hurting the other person at all. This relationship is illustrated in 3-c.

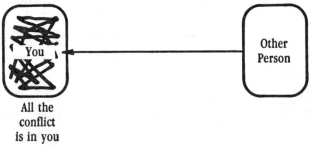

**Illustration 3-c**

A person can only handle so much hurt, repressed feelings, conflict, and anger. If conflict ends up being internalized, it will eventually have to find a way out. The end result will not only be that you are hurt, but also that you will hurt the person you are trying to avoid having a conflict with, who is usually someone close to you. This backlash of emotions is depicted in Illustration 3-d.

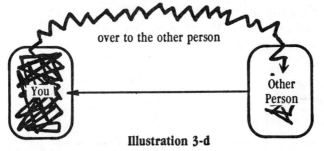

So much conflict that it spills

over to the other person

You

Other Person

**Illustration 3-d**

Another option that some people take is to push the conflict onto the other person. This relationship is illustrated in 3-e. They are living out the philosophy, "Do your own thing, and if the other person doesn't like it, that's tough."

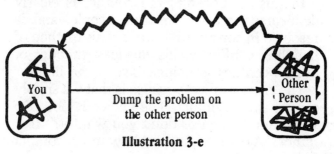

You

Other Person

Dump the problem on the other person

**Illustration 3-e**

In essence, they are "dumping" on the other person. This often works for a while—that is, if the dumper can find someone who will take it. But guess what happens—the other person will tolerate all he can, but sooner or later it will splash back one way or another.

In retrospect, the important thing to note is that the least amount of conflict feasible for a person was illustrated in 3-a, which is rediagramed below.

Least amount of conflict

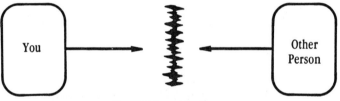

Conflict is out in the open

**Illustration 3-a**

In this relationship, the conflict is clearly delineated between the two people, and is resolved in constructive ways. This method of handling conflict yields the least amount of overall conflict, emotional stress, and illness.

The crucial thing to realize is that we simply cannot avoid conflict. The choice is not "Do you want conflict or don't you want it?" It is rather "Where, when, and how much conflict do you want?'' We do not have the option of avoiding conflict. Conflict is a fact of life. But we do have the choice as to how we will handle it and what the long-range results will be. The choice is not one of turmoil or no turmoil; it is a choice of the intensity of the turmoil and the duration of the turmoil.

During a person's earlier years he may have been able to repress his feelings quite adequately, so that his life could go on fairly comfortably. However, as he grows older there will build within him such a large unresolved anger fund that emotional and physical symptoms will become inevitable. If you take the emotionally easy way out now, it will eventually catch up to you with sizable accumulated interest.

### *Confrontation Is Necessary*

Bringing conflict out into the open and dealing with it constructively can be termed confrontation. Again, this is something that many people avoid at all costs—and the costs are high.

I'm reminded of a 14-year-old boy whose parents allow him to control them to such a degree that they will do almost anything he requests. Occasionally he will have to get fairly angry before they will cater to his wishes, but most of the time they yield without much resistance. They came to me for help but would allow the boy to stop treatment at any time. The boy had his parents moving from one state to another because he felt he would be happier in another location. I remember the day I requested that he have a blood test to be sure there was no physical basis for his emotional difficulty. Before an hour had passed, I had received a phone call from both parents. The boy had created such a fuss over the recommended blood test that the father was called home from work.

To this day the situation remains unchanged. He has never submitted to the simple blood test to rule out the possibility that an endocrine disease may be causing his emotional difficulty. Unfortunately, the price being paid by the parents and the boy is tremendous. He is having extreme difficulty in school, and unless there is a drastic change soon, these demanding traits will characterize his adult life. But because his parents are afraid of confronting him, they are continuing to yield to his destructive demands.

Several weeks ago I saw a new patient—a successful, middle-aged business woman who was seriously considering death rather than a moderate degree of emotional conflict. She was considering jumping off a pier to avoid confronting a problem with her husband about how to raise their teenage son.

I've seen many people avoid at all costs the thought of confronting another individual. The idea of dealing with their own feelings or someone else's in a constructive, direct fashion is extremely uncomfortable to them. They protest that they can't stand an "argument" and will do anything to avoid it. And so they suffer the long-term consequences. In reality, it is like refusing a painful injection of penicillin, preferring to suffer with pneumonia despite the effects. Unfortunately, there are many people with emotional pneumonia, so to speak, who prefer to endure the illness rather than take the necessary prescription because it hurts too much, though only for a moment.

You might ask, "Why is it that so many people do not really confront issues directly and constructively?" I think there are a number of reasons. First of all, dealing with anger constructively is often more uncomfortable at first than dealing with it destructively. It takes time and effort to deal with anger in a positive way, especially when first learning how.

Secondly, many people have been taught that "standing up to others" is wrong. They have gotten the impression that nice, compliant, religious people accept things meekly. They may get so much praise for being such a "nice" person that they find it very hard to mar that image. Some people have seen confrontations done in an aggressive, hostile manner, so they shun *all* confrontations. There are also those who just don't know how to confront. They have never been taught how to handle anger properly and haven't had a model to learn from. Individuals with a large unresolved anger fund will find it very difficult to learn how to handle their anger calmly because they are perpetually hovering near the boiling point.

Lastly, many people don't fully grasp the long-term consequences of failing to confront those with whom they are angry, so they continue on in their old ways.

All of us know from past experience that it is a great deal easier to destroy than to build. It takes effort, planning, and a lot of work to build good relationships, and many people are just not willing to put forth that effort. As you start to face the anger problem in your life, things at first may seem to get worse before they get better. If you are the type of person who is overtly angry, you will have to learn to control yourself in order to confront the problem constructively. You may have to give up the momentary pleasure that comes from hurting other people.

If you are the type of person who avoids confrontations, you will have to give up your tendency to withdraw—to pull in your feelings instead of dealing with them. You'll also have to learn to deal with the other person's feelings. Either way, these new behavior patterns will be difficult to learn because they run contrary to how you have been acting instinctively all these years.

Things may indeed get worse before they get better. I wish I could tell you otherwise—I wish I could offer you an instant-success formula—but I wouldn't be honest if I did.

However, in every case that I know of, things have improved significantly in the long run for those who have had the courage to learn how to handle anger constructively and have persevered. I don't know of a single person who has applied the principles in this book who has failed to profit considerably from them.

In Illustration 4-a, I have tried to demonstrate the principle that dealing constructively with anger may initially cause

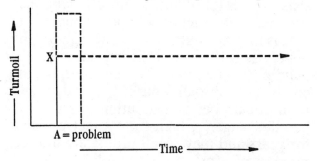

**Illustration 4-a**

more discomfort than dealing with it destructively. The vertical axis represents the increase of turmoil in a person's life. The horizontal axis indicates the passage of time. At the point marked A, a problem is encountered and the person senses conflict and feelings of hurt or anger. But at the point designated with an X, he is confronted with a choice. This is the moment the person realizes that there is a problem and has to decide how to handle it. If he decides to handle it constructively, the turmoil increases, as illustrated by the dotted line. Note that at first there is an increase in the turmoil, which is then followed by a resolution. However, if this person is unwilling to bear any increase in emotional discomfort, he can take the "easy way out," as illustrated by the dashed line. The emotionally easy way out often results in the problem never being resolved, so at some level the turmoil persists indefinitely. This is typically what happens with destructively handled anger.

This may be somewhat oversimplified, but hopefully it illustrates the crucial point that handling anger properly may be quite uncomfortable initially, but it generally results in a much better resolution than poorly handled anger, which may affect our lives for years and may result ultimately in much more discomfort.

To illustrate this phenomenon further, let's take the hypothetical case of a person who has had five anger-producing situations arise in a period of a month. Illustration 4-b shows how this might look on a chart for the person who handles his problems constructively.

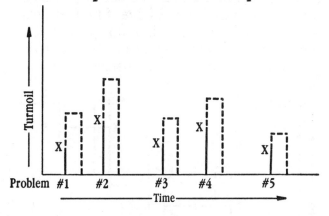

**Illustration 4-b**

Again, we have the same factors as in Illustration 4-a. Turmoil is on the vertical axis and time is on the horizontal axis, but this time there are five opportunities for confrontations. In each confrontation there is a choice: whether to deal with the conflict constructively or destructively. In Illustration 4-b, the individual chooses to deal with each problem constructively as it arises.

However, what would have happened if this person had the same five problems but handled each of them destructively? This is illustrated in 4-c. With Problem #1, there is some immediate turmoil, but at point X no choice is made to deal with the problem constructively. Note that the turmoil doesn't increase immediately or rise to the height that it would have if he had dealt with it constructively, but notice also that the turmoil never decreased, nor was the problem ever resolved. It just went on and on and on.

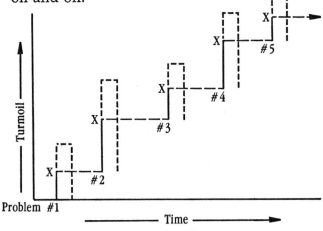

**Illustration 4-c**

So when Problem #2 hits, it's superimposed on the residual turmoil from Problem #1. Again he is faced with a decision: "Do I deal with this one constructively or do I take the easy road out?" See what happens if he makes the latter choice—a repeat of the pattern of #1, only at a higher level of turmoil.

Through each of the five problems, if he continues to take the easy way out, the chronic turmoil in his life increases. Can you imagine the amount of hurt, buried anger, and troubled relationships that can build in a person's lifetime if he repeatedly handles anger-producing situations destructively? I see people like that professionally, and it is no small feat to reverse this pattern.

Fortunately, some people do learn to reverse this pattern. Recently I received a letter from a past patient. She was a Christian elementary-school teacher in her late twenties when she first started seeing me several years ago. She was suicidal and unable to teach or go to graduate school. She was totally unaware of any anger in her life. I was seeing her weekly for about two years, and one of the major items we worked on was helping her get in touch with her feelings, especially hurt and angry feelings.

She progressed very well and stopped therapy about five months ago. In her letter, she told about the many accomplishments in her life. She is a third-grade teacher, working with some moderately rough kids. She wrote, "My biggest struggle was being firm with the boys. This often led to getting irritated (notice "irritated," not angry) and for awhile there I felt awful. But now I feel no guilt in getting upset with them while being firm because it is helping them and myself."

Anger can be likened to a fire in a fireplace in a remote cabin during a blizzard. If the fire gets out of control, it will destroy the occupants, either directly by the fire itself or indirectly when they flee and are exposed to the blizzard. On the other hand, if the fire goes out, the occupants will freeze within the cabin. The key, then, is adequate respect for the fire, and adequate control and channeling of it.

So it is with feelings of anger. Anger can be a very valuable force if put to constructive use in our lives. It can actually be a positive motivating power. However, many people have trouble accepting themselves and their feelings, and thus they find it difficult to acknowledge their own anger. But if they could learn to deal with anger, even though dealing with it is uncomfortable and has some unpleasant components, they would discover that it is a powerful agent that can be used constructively in their lives and in the lives of those around them.

In summary, it is important to mention that one of the main reasons people avoid dealing with anger is that they think expressing it will hurt relationships with other people. But the opposite is true. If you don't admit to being hurt or angry and don't express your anger in constructive ways, you may eventually destroy relationships and hurt at least one of the people involved.

It is a fact that people can handle constructively expressed hurt or anger much better than repressed or camouflaged forms of anger. Failing to deal constructively with anger may in the long run destroy the love that was once there, because if you repress feelings of anger, you will inevitably squelch all feelings, especially feelings of love. I might add that if you find yourself incapable of feeling love toward anyone, it may well be because there is a large unresolved anger fund that has not been dealt with.

On the other hand, when we express our honest feelings in constructive ways, true love is never killed but strengthened. Expressing anger constructively will never damage a worthwhile relationship. If a relationship is destroyed by attempting to deal constructively with angry feelings, it was probably a sick relationship to start with, and not much was lost.

Confronting the other person should not be construed as a sign of hostility; rather, it indicates that you care enough about the person to work out the problems in the relationship, no matter how painful the process may be. When you express feelings honestly, it means that you respect and value yourself and the other person. Expressing one's deepest feelings can in fact be a very cleansing experience, one in which the love and respect shared between the two people is usually strengthened. In addition, the other person will think more highly of you, and your own self-esteem will increase.

# Chapter

# Six

## *Handling Your Anger*

All of these theories about anger are fine, but what are you supposed to do when you actually get angry? What are you supposed to do when someone snaps at you or insults you, and suddenly you feel hurt, your jaw tenses, and angry retorts flash through your head?

I have outlined a step-by-step procedure to draw upon in problem situations like this.

### *Recognize Your Feelings of Displeasure*

The first step is to get in touch with your feelings of hurt, displeasure, or anger. For many people this is not a problem because they are acutely aware of their feelings. However, for a large segment of society this first step is the most important one. They may be like Jan, the person described in the first chapter who contemplated jumping off the Vincent Thomas Bridge in San Pedro. She had repressed her feelings of anger for so long that its only manifestation was that she felt funny and confused. Only after we had spent almost 30 minutes reconstructing the events that led to this aimless confusion did it become apparent that she had been feeling slight irritation.

I have worked with several individuals like Jan with whom it has taken several years of therapy for them to get in touch with their feelings. Typically in a therapy session we would examine the resultant manifestations of the anger and then would have to work back to the initial feelings. Sometimes even after all that, they still wouldn't feel anything. Then we would have to look at the situation and see how they handled it in order to discover what kinds of feelings might have produced their behavior. At other times we would try to figure out what other people might feel in a similar situation.

Usually I have to search for and use exactly the right word to describe their feelings. For example, if I use a word like "mad," "angry," or "furious," they often reject it. However, if I use the word "annoyed," it might be accepted as an appropriate term to describe their feelings. The third-grade teacher described in the previous chapter always rejected the word "anger" and denied any feeling of anger, but some of the time she could identify "slight feelings of irritation." So we would work with "feelings of irritation" in applying the principles of this book. By these means, then, we are able to fan the embers of their feelings until they become stronger.

At this point in the proceedings, *do not judge* the cause of the feeling as to whether it is reasonable or not, or even as to whether it is right or wrong. Here you are identifying the presence of any hurt or anger feelings only. This step can be compared to looking at the temperature gauge on the dashboard of your car; you aren't determining the cause of the overheated engine, but are only aware of the fact that it is overheated.

While you are getting in touch with your feelings of displeasure, evaluate just how upset you really are. Try to determine whether you are a little upset, moderately upset, or very upset. This will serve as an important clue later on as to the action you may need to take. Also, if you don't appreciate the degree of your anger, you may find yourself overreacting to minor issues or even underreacting to major ones.

### Suppress Taking Any Action

The second step is to suppress taking any action until you have *thought through* the situation and have *control* of what you say and do. Suppressing taking action is not the same as repression. When a person represses anger, he buries it and often isn't aware of the feelings at all. However, suppressing anger means that you defer taking action without losing touch with the problem. It is akin to the proverbial "counting to ten." Sometimes this step may take only seconds or minutes, but in some cases it may take hours or possibly days.

The Bible encourages us not to be hasty in dealing with our anger. Proverbs 29:11 says, "A fool gives full vent to his anger, but a wise man quietly holds it back" (RSV). The Amplified Bible says, "A self-confident fool utters all his anger, but a wise man keeps it back and stills it."

I have already stated that I would not take any action at this stage in the proceedings. However, there are two exceptions. If you find yourself in a situation in which you suddenly have some angry feelings that aren't altogether clear to you yet, and someone asks you if you're upset, the temptation will be to say, "No, it didn't bother me." If in reality you were bothered, saying that you weren't would be dishonest, and it makes it more difficult to deal with the incident with that person later on, should the need arise.

It would be better to say something like, "Yes, what you said did upset me, but I'll have to think it through before I say anything more about it." Or you might tag the situation by saying, "Something about that bothers me, but it's not clear to me yet. Maybe when I've had a chance to think it over we can talk about it." Tagging the situation marks it as a problem to you and the other person, but are consciously deferring any definitive action. It also alerts the other person to think about what was said and done, and decreases the chance that he will forget about it, which might further anger you, making dealing with it more difficult.

If you don't tag the situation verbally, it is crucial that you at least tag it in your mind. As a result, if there are some urgent tasks at hand when you become aware that something is bothering you, you will have pinned the problem down in your mind and committed yourself to coming back to deal with it later. If you don't tag the situation, it is very possible that you will forget the specific issue that caused you to feel upset. Then if you feel vaguely upset later, you won't know why and you may be unable to resolve the problem. Doing this repeatedly can cause all kinds of havoc and can add to your unresolved anger fund.

Several months ago my wife suggested that I take over a certain responsibility around the house that she had been handling up to that time. Immediately I became aware that this suggestion irritated me, and a score of considerations passed rapidly through my mind. Does she have a legitimate basis for asking me to do this? I do so many other things, and I'm so busy right now with my schedule, etc., etc., etc. Because she can read my facial expressions, she asked, "Did that bother you?" I responded, "Yes, it upset me."

Thus I tagged the situation, and while I honestly thought I would be able to sort out my feelings fairly quickly, it took at least another ten minutes for my thoughts to get clarified on the issue. Then when they were clarified, I could express my feelings and we were able to work through the problem. In this situation I followed the first two steps in dealing with anger: I recognized my feelings of displeasure and I suppressed taking any action, though I tagged the situation.

One additional thing that you may want to do is to notify innocent bystanders when something is on your mind. Thus if you have had a very traumatic day at work and you come home with a lot of things on your mind, it is wise to inform your family that you've had a difficult day and to ask them to give you some room. When you let them know that they are not the ones who are troubling you, they are less likely to conjure up a thousand and one reasons for your behavior. Instead of making them feel responsible for your bad mood, they are more likely to be helpful, if by doing nothing more than staying out of your way.

However, informing them of your dilemma never gives you license to take out your frustrations on them. Also, if asking your family for "room" occurs very frequently, you may need to take a deeper look as to why this is occurring so often and what the effects are on your family.

It also pays to remember that timing is very important in dealing with emotional issues. I've already mentioned that it is essential to wait before taking action until you have thought through the situation and have adequate control of both your words and actions. I want to emphasize that I am not saying that you must have control of all of your feelings, whether primary or secondary feelings. In fact, at times it is useful to take action when there are still some feelings present, because they can help you take the necessary action. It is also a very valuable experience for our children to see us handle anger appropriately when we are visibly upset.

However, I'm not at all suggesting the expression of excessive anger by extreme means. A patient once told me about an incident that is applicable to this issue. This lady had had many psychiatric hospitalizations, and one of the contributing factors to her problem was an uncooperative, fully grown son who had been freeloading off her for years. Once when she was feeling worse and was going to be admitted to a psychiatric hospital, her son seemed very pleased at the prospect of getting rid of her as he brought her bags to the car. This made her so furious that she marched back into the house with her suitcases and told her son to get out of the house and support himself.

This may not have been the most mature way to handle the problem, but for her it was progress, and it is a graphic example of how emotional energy can be used in positive ways. This same thing happened when the Spirit of God came upon Saul, causing him to become very angry and to move into action (1 Samuel 11:6,7).

In this step of suppressing taking action (because we don't want to take premature action), we don't want to delay unnecessarily either. Every minute that unresolved conflict is carried inside, it extracts a tremendous toll on a person's life. Thus you should suppress taking action until the above criteria are met, but thereafter action should be taken as soon as possible. At first, learning to identify your feelings and thinking through the situation may take days, weeks, or even months. But later you will be able to go through this step more quickly, usually at the time of the initial hurt.

### Pray

Particularly in stressful situations (as we have been discussing), it would seem appropriate to mention how helpful a prayerful attitude of dependency on God can be. Simply stating, "Lord, help me see the issues more clearly" or "Lord, help me sort out my thoughts and feelings so I can do the right thing" cannot be overemphasized.

I don't believe that a person necessarily has to pray specifically in each and every little situation that arises, but I do believe this should be the general desire of the heart. On the other hand, there may be many occasions in which a person will want to draw away from the crowd to pray specifically about a situation.

### Identify the Cause of Your Anger

What is it that is making you feel upset or angry? What is causing your anger? What is the primary feeling that is leading to the angry feelings? What is being threatened?

Answering these questions is the next step. Many times the cause of the anger is very obvious, so this step is no problem at all.

However, people who have difficulty understanding and dealing with their feelings may have considerable difficulty with this step. If you get angry at your ten-year-old son for leaving his bike in the driveway, you need to consider whether you are really angry with your child or whether the true cause of your anger is the boss who chewed you out at work or the man who cut you off on the freeway or some combination thereof. Anger can so easily be displaced to someone or something with whom it is safer to express that bottled-up feeling. I'm sure you are all familiar with the following chain reaction: The boss yelled at his employee, who then got angry at his wife, who then took it out on her son, who in turn kicked the dog.

This procedure of taking out one's anger on a weaker creature is not unique to human beings; it has even been documented in laboratory animals. Probably the first recorded incident of the displacement of anger onto a defenseless animal is found in Numbers 22, where Balaam became angry at his donkey instead of realizing that he was upset because God wouldn't cooperate with his plan.

I know of people who are stymied at this step because they have difficulty in figuring out what made them so angry. Each of them in his or her own way has to pause to determine the sequence of events leading up to the anger. One person will have to take a piece of paper and start writing until the issues are clarified. Another may have to talk over the problem with a close friend. Still another may need professional help to identify the source of his angry feelings. But whatever it takes to do the job, you cannot proceed any further until the cause of the displeasure is identified.

In real-life situations there is often more than one issue to which we must respond. One of my patients had her mother say to her, "That certainly is a beautiful dress, even if you are overweight." Here the mother was sending out two distinctly different messages in one sentence. Let's look at the problems that could develop if the daughter doesn't separate and deal with both parts of the message. One response might be for her to express appreciation for the compliment about the dress but to ignore the put-down about her weight. Here she is apt to feel quite angry about the latter comment, and this anger in turn is likely to be pushed into her unresolved anger fund.

The second way she might respond is to deal only with the second part of the message, saying something like, "It sure makes me mad when you criticize me about my weight.'' The mother might then respond, ''Well, I was just trying to pay you a compliment. Can't I even say anything nice to you?'' Thus the mother is reacting only as if she is complimenting the daughter, but the daughter is reacting only as if she is being criticized. Then they are apt to get into an argument in which each is arguing about a different thing and in which neither of their feelings is resolved.

Dealing with only one part of the message is quite inadequate and causes all sorts of havoc. The daughter has to separate the contradictory messages, both the compliment and the insult. She must then decide if and how she wants to respond to both parts of this message. Here she might say, ''Thanks for the compliment about the dress, but your comment about my weight really irritated me.'' From that point on they can deal with either or both of the issues.

In this illustration, the fact that there are two different issues is quite obvious. Unfortunately, most situations are not quite as obvious. When several messages are being sent and when they are more subtle than in this illustration, sorting them out and dealing with each one becomes a difficult process.

Also, when a person attempts to deal honestly with himself, sometimes another facet of the problem may emerge. He may have to sort out to what degree he is responsible for the problem and to what degree the other person is responsible. Then he will need to deal with each of those aspects appropriately. This will be discussed in more detail later.

## *Is Your Anger Legitimate?*

Nehemiah said, "I was very angry when I heard their cry and these words. I thought it over, then rebuked the nobles and officials" (Nehemiah 5:6,7 AMP). Here Nehemiah was able to get in touch with his feelings, to think through the situation, and then to take the appropriate action of rebuking the leaders. Elsewhere in the Scriptures we find, "Then God said to Jonah, 'Do you have good reason to be angry?' " (Jonah 4:9). In this case God was questioning Jonah as to whether he had an adequate basis for his angry feelings. It turned out that Jonah didn't have just cause for his anger.

This reminds me of the day my 13-year-old son came whizzing past me in the breakfast room and greeted me with the words, "Hi, Chubby." He wasn't even out of the room by the time I could sense that I was hurt and starting to get angry. I was just about ready to say something when I realized that there was some truth in what he had just said, so I delayed taking any action.

As I thought about it, I became aware that the legitimacy of the statement was what made it hurt; what made me so mad was the fact that he was right. I had been telling myself for the past six months that I should be working on my weight. Thus I concluded that he was right and that I had no legitimate basis for getting upset with him, and soon my feelings of hurt and anger quickly subsided. If he had a habit of saying things like that it would have been a different matter, but this had been the only time he had ever made such a comment, and so I could let it pass.

It is interesting to note that within a week a colleague of mine at work said to me, "You ought to lose some weight, Dwight." This time I was able to agree with him, saying, "You know, you're right." And this feeling of displeasure with my weight spurred me on to losing 20 pounds.

### Determine a Course of Action

At any of the above steps, you may have been able to resolve the problem. If that is the case, so much the better, and the steps that follow will not be necessary for you. However, if the problem is not resolved, then you will need to take further action to handle your feelings constructively, lest they turn into a destructive force against you or others.

Most people deal with conflict by one of the following methods: 1) They angrily attack—"I'll get even with him"; 2) they run or withdraw—"I'll take my marbles and go home"; 3) they verbally give in to the other person—"Okay, you win"; but in reality they are unhappy with the situation. People who use the latter two methods typically harbor resentment. Finally, there is a fourth method in which there is a total denial of any conflict. This person may not even be aware that a conflict exists, which only magnifies the problem by making handling the conflict extremely difficult.

In spite of the fact that all of the above methods are grossly inadequate in dealing with conflicts, many people still rely heavily upon them. What people really need to know is that there is a large array of skills available to them for the handling of situations in which there is conflict. They need to become proficient in selecting the best means of handling a given situation. The following are specific courses of action that one can take when conflict arises.

### *Confront When Necessary*

Anyone who really cares about people and their feelings finds confrontation difficult, but a mature person will confront someone when it is necessary. In 2 Corinthians 2:4 Paul shares with his readers how he felt about having to confront them: "Oh, how I hated to write that letter! It almost broke my heart, and I tell you honestly that I cried over it. I didn't want to hurt you, but I had to show you how very much I loved you and cared about what was happening to you" (TLB).

It is worthwhile here to take a brief look at the context of the previously quoted verse about anger, Ephesians 4:26, noting particularly verses 25-27,32: "Therefore, laying aside falsehood, speak truth, each one of you, with his neighbor, for we are members of one another. Be angry, and yet do not sin; do not let the sun go down on your anger, and do not give the devil an opportunity . . . . Be kind to one another, tenderhearted, forgiving . . . ." In other words, first there is the call to drop the mask of falsehood and to speak the truth to each other, but be honest with each other. Then the writer of this passage states that though anger is called for in some situations, we must not let it lead to sin. He then goes on to tell us to be kind and tenderhearted to each other, and to forgive each other.

At first glance these instructions may appear to contradict each other, but when seen in the light of dealing honestly with anger, the entire perspective changes. Speaking the truth in love often necessitates confrontation, and sometimes this confrontation must take place before one can be tender and forgiving. In his book *Caring Enough to Confront,* David Augsburger speaks of confrontation as "truthing it in love."

There are many examples of confrontation in the Scriptures. Probably the first example that comes to mind is when Jesus sharply attacked the Pharisees in Mark 7. It is interesting to note that even Jesus' disciples couldn't understand His remarks to the religious leaders, and on one occasion they came to Him and said, "You offended the Pharisees by that remark" (Matthew 15:12 TLB). But Jesus did not retract His statements because He had fully intended to confront them.

Jesus also rebuked Peter sharply in Matthew 16:23. We find that Paul "had great dissension and debate" with some men from Judea regarding religious customs (Acts 15:2). Paul also opposed Peter "to his face" because Peter was wrong on a certain issue (Galatians 2:11).

Confrontation isn't necessarily a hostile, painful experience; it can also be done in a tender and forgiving manner. One example of this kind of confrontation is the way Jesus treated the adulterous woman whom the Pharisees wanted to stone to death. Jesus told the Pharisees, "Let him who is without sin among you cast the first stone." One by one the Pharisees slipped away. Jesus then turned to the woman and said, "Where are your accusers? . . . Go, and sin no more" (John 8).

Jesus had a similarly gentle confrontation with the woman He met at the well, who was living with someone to whom she wasn't married. He didn't gloss over the fact that what she was doing was wrong, but He also introduced her to a new way of living (John 4). Genuine confrontation, "truthing it in love," is not attacking another person, but caring enough about the person and the relationship to talk directly to him.

Whenever possible, it is best that confrontation be done in private. If a problem has developed between you and another individual, endeavor to resolve it between the two of you alone, without involving others. Proverbs 25:8,9 says, "Do not go out hastily to argue your case; otherwise what will you do in the end, when your neighbor puts you to shame? Argue your case with your neighbor, and do not reveal the secret of another." Matthew 18:15 says, "If a brother sins against you, go to him privately and confront him with his fault" (TLB).

There are several exceptions to this. First, if others have observed the conflict or were in some way involved, it may need to be resolved with these individuals present. Another time that you may want to involve others is if a person refuses to deal with you alone, yet you feel that an important principle or issue is at stake that requires resolution. The passage in Matthew 18:15 continues, "If he listens and confesses it, you have won back a brother. But if not, then take one or two others with you and go back to him again, proving everything you say by these witnesses. If he still refuses to listen, then take your case to the church" (verses 16, 17 TLB). Though it is preferable not to involve others, there are some occasions when it is necessary, as when the problem can't be resolved adequately without them.

Confrontation can thus vary widely from a very gentle, private resolution of an issue to a strong, possibly unpleasant situation involving others. There are three general ways to confront people: 1) to inform; 2) to share your primary feelings; and 3) to rebuke in love.

On January 29, 1979, an Air Force sergeant traveling from California to Colorado spent more money than anticipated on car repairs. Consequently, he ran out of gas and money in Raton, New Mexico. Although he had money in his checking account, the banks, gas stations, and motels refused his personal checks. So the sergeant obediently went to his disabled car, where he spent the night in subfreezing weather. Had the police department or others in the town been informed of his plight, they would have made provisions for him, as they had for others in the past. But the sergeant's failure to inform the townspeople of his situation cost him his feet, which had to be amputated because they were so badly frostbitten. This situation brought grief not only to the sergeant, but to the residents of the town as well. This incident graphically illustrates the extent to which people can be hurt simply because they fail to adequately inform others of their situation.

We often overlook or fail to inform another person clearly and honestly about our feelings on an issue that affects us. For example, the simple statement "You're stepping on my foot" is usually the best way to inform a person in a crowded elevator that he is hurting you and that you would like him to stop. Often the person isn't even aware that he is stepping on your foot unless you quietly inform him of the fact. To angrily snap, "You're stepping on my foot, you clod!" only complicates the situation. Another example of informing is saying to the person who cuts in front of you, "The line forms over there." Even if the person has deliberately taken advantage of you, usually a simple statement resolves the situation effectively.

When we feel something strongly, it is up to us to express it. *We are asking for all kinds of trouble if we assume that the other person knows how strongly we feel, unless we actually put it into words and express our feelings directly to the person involved.*

My wife and I have been guilty in the past of inadequately informing each other of our feelings, and we continue to find it necessary to work on this area of our marriage. I recall an incident that occurred nine years ago that made us acutely aware of the need to share our feelings. I was extremely busy with a full practice and was on many hospital and church-related committees. Often I would leave home early in the morning, before the family had breakfast, and would arrive home late at night, after everyone was in bed. No doubt I was in error for being so busy, and for that reason I was not tuned in to Betty's needs. Betty, on the other hand, not wanting to bother me with her needs because I was so busy, only hinted quietly of her need to talk with me, hints which I honestly didn't hear. If I had received her messages more clearly, I would have dropped almost anything to be of help to her, but I had no idea how much she was hurting, and she didn't know how to inform me.

One day a friend confronted Betty with her responsibility to inform me of her turmoil, even if it meant making an appointment with me in my office. Finally Betty wrote me a note and left it on my desk to open the channels of communication, but unfortunately she went through some very painful weeks before she informed me, and by that time it had created some deep hurts for both of us. Had I recognized it or had she informed me earlier, it would have saved both of us a lot of grief.

The second way to confront is to *convey your primary feelings.* Anger itself is a secondary feeling or reaction to some insult, threat, put-down, or frustration of our wishes. The initial or primary feeling is hurt, belittlement, or frustration, to name a few typical ones. For example, if someone stomps on your foot, you first feel pain, which is followed by anger and the urge to push the person off your foot. Each step in this God-given process is vital. The primary feeling of pain is the protective warning signal. The secondary feeling, anger, enables you to take protective actions against the offender. One of the most constructive ways of dealing with anger is to get in touch with the primary feeling and then to share this with the person you need to confront.

This is best exemplified by sending an "I feel" message. "I feel" messages are a beautiful way of sharing how you feel, and they often help everyone involved to get in touch with their primary feelings. Below are some examples of "I feel" messages, as contrasted to "Blaming you" messages.

| "I Feel" Messages | "Blaming You" Messages |
| --- | --- |
| 1. I'm feeling ignored. | You're making me mad because you're paying so much attention to Mary. |
| 2. I feel disappointed that I can't go too. | You're making me angry by deliberately leaving me behind. |
| 3. I get the feeling that I'm being blamed for that. | You always blame me for everything that goes wrong. |
| 4. I feel put down. | You're always putting me down. |
| 5. I feel like I'm being interrogated. | Why are you finding fault with me again? |

In contrast to the "I feel" messages, "Blaming you" messages usually begin with the word "you" and often include an accusation. They frequently assume to know the intent, motivation, and feelings of the other person. Even if the "Blaming you" message is correct, it is usually difficult to defend. Such messages come off as being judgmental, critical, attacking, and final, giving no room for the other person. They tend to raise the hostilities and defenses of the other person, a process which often happens unconsciously. Only the extremely mature person can receive a "Blaming you" message and turn it into a constructive interaction.

During my psychiatric residency, I was eating lunch once with several colleagues when my boss sat down and joined us. During the course of the conversation he said something that really hurt me and made me feel very insulted. In my mind I quickly went through the steps mentioned earlier, and within about two seconds I was aware of intense hurt and angry feelings, and I knew I needed to confront him. I said just two words—"That hurts." For about a minute, you could have heard a pin drop at that table. The topic of conversation changed, but later I sought him out to share in greater depth my honest feelings with him and to ask him some specific questions regarding his. The problem was resolved between us.

Another incident occurred at about the same period of time which involved a colleague of mine and a supervising psychiatrist. On other occasions it appeared to me that this supervisor had torn into other residents unmercifully. He seemed to be throwing out disguised criticisms at my colleague and me because we hadn't gotten some more problem patients to discuss with him. I certainly didn't want him to tear into me, but neither did I like the anger I was beginning to feel toward him. So I said, "I'm beginning to feel uncomfortable," and then said nothing for awhile. Again there was dead silence for probably 30 or 40 seconds, after which he said, "Now I'm beginning to feel uncomfortable." I still said nothing further, and then he quickly interjected, "I didn't mean any criticism by what I said." Thus the problem was resolved by sending an "I feel" message. I might add that during the rest of the time everything went well, without any feelings of being criticized.

I would heartily encourage you to read *Caring Enough to Confront,* by David Augsburger. He discusses the "I feel" messages under the heading of "I" messages. On page 25 he says, "Avoiding honest statements of real feelings and viewpoints is often considered kindness, thoughtfulness, or generosity. More often it is the most cruel thing I can do to others. It is a kind of benevolent lying."

The third and strongest way to confront is to *rebuke in love.* Here you are telling the person directly that what he is saying or doing is inappropriate, but note that the rebuke is given in love, which differentiates it from the angry attack. Because you care about the person you are rebuking, the aim of rebuking in love is reconciliation. You may dislike or even hate what the person is doing, but you do care about the person. Proverbs 27:5,6 says, "Open rebuke is better than hidden love! Wounds from a friend are better than kisses from an enemy!" (TLB). Eli probably sinned because "he did not rebuke" his sons. He only meekly questioned them when they disregarded God's laws of worship (1 Samuel 3:13).

One word of warning regarding confrontation: Some people are afraid of confronting someone because they don't know if they will be able to control their anger. For most people, learning to confront others is very uncomfortable at first. But despite the disconcerting feelings that accompany confrontations, very few people end up physically or verbally attacking the other person if they have thought through the steps listed previously. However, if someone feels violently angry, he may have to put off confrontation and get some help, perhaps even professional help, so that he will eventually be able to confront the person without physically harming him.

I treated a man like this for several years. He had an extreme rage toward his father, and I discouraged him from confronting his father until he had dissipated some of his anger in psychotherapy. However, please don't use the above caution as an excuse for avoiding confrontation.

### *Establish Limits of Behavior*

Kristine, a 31-year-old patient of mine, sought my help because of depression. She has two boys, ages eight and ten, with whom she is frequently angry. For example, John, the ten-year-old, frequently leaves his bicycle outside the back door, requiring others to walk around it. Several times Kristine stumbled over it. Kristine is aware of her anger over this and she certainly confronts John, but it is with yelling and screaming, and it doesn't seem to be accomplishing very much.

Last week we talked about setting limits on what is and what is not acceptable behavior, and how to utilize appropriate consequences. Guess what—the next day Kristine was carrying a large box from the house to the garage, and she didn't see John's bike. She stumbled and dropped the box. As the adrenalin started to surge, so did her yelling.

Then she remembered our session of the previous day. Her rage decreased and she firmly called John. She explained what had just happened and how she might have injured herself or damaged items in the box. Then she clearly and firmly told John that she would take the box to the garage and that she expected the bike to be removed by the time she returned. If it wasn't removed, she would remove it; and if she ever had to take that action again the bike would be locked up for a week. This would mean he would have to walk a mile-and-a-half to and from school and wouldn't be able to play with his bike after school—something very important to him.

As Kristine walked to the garage she was amazed at how quickly her angry feelings had subsided. Normally this would have ruined the rest of her day, and possibly also the day for the entire family. When she returned to the house the bike was gone, and it has not been left at the back door since then. Kristine was amazed at how well this resolved the problem, as compared with her previous habit of yelling. She had established a limit of behavior with predetermined consequences, which negated her anger and produced the desired results.

Limit-setting with predetermined consequences can be used in any situation in which one has the right and/or responsibility over others. This is especially applicable with parents, teachers, and employers. Keep in mind, however, that when setting limits the rules or limits should be fair and consistently applied, all parties should know the consequences before the infraction is done, and the limit-setter must follow through on the consequences even though there may be the temptation to make "just one exception." Most of the time the rule-setting can be done when you don't feel angry, and this will be covered in Chapter 9.

In most instances it isn't wise to establish the consequences after the offense. For example, if Kristine had stumbled on John's bike and had locked it without warning him, he might have had legitimate reason to feel that his mother was unfair. In this situation she was angry, she set the limits, she gave him enough time to meet them, and she let him know that the consequences would be applied immediately for any future infraction of the rule.

For further help in setting limits I would suggest Dr. James Dobson's books *Dare to Discipline* and *The Strong-Willed Child*.

### Get Counsel

Another way to handle negative feelings is to seek counsel. At times all of us find ourselves in need of someone with whom we can talk over a problem. This person need not be a professional; sometimes a friend, spouse, or peer who can help clarify issues and give objectivity to a problem is all that we need. In any case, this person should be fairly mature and a good listener, and shouldn't be prone to give quick answers.

He should be a confidant who won't gossip about your problem or use it against you. Some people may need to get counsel from a professional. This is especially true of a person who might lose control of himself if he started getting in touch with his anger or other deep feelings. As mentioned previously, praying is certainly advisable at this point and can be an invaluable means of getting counsel from God, the Great Counselor (see James 1:5).

### Talk Things Out

Catharsis is closely related to getting counsel. It means to cleanse or purge, to talk things out. Since it is the healthy release of ideas and feelings, especially the painful ones, this step may need to precede the above step because some people may need to "get it all out" before any counsel can be effective. Usually catharsis is thought of as talking things out in the presence of another person, someone who knows how to listen emphatically. For some people, sharing their deepest feelings to God in prayer is an excellent means of catharsis. For others, psychotherapy may be necessary. However, I have seen people get things out of their system by writing a letter, even if they never mail it. Others may put their thoughts on paper, talk to themselves in private, or even record their feelings on a cassette recorder. In some instances catharsis is all that is needed to dissipate one's hurt and angry feelings. In other situations, however, it is only one of several steps that need to be taken.

### Compromise When Appropriate

Seldom when we get angry are we 100 percent right and the other person 100 percent wrong. Typically, there are multiple factors causing the problem and several different ways to view the situation. Often after we have gone through some of the steps for handling anger, particularly the step of confrontation, we become aware of the other person's feelings, and suddenly we are faced with a different perspective on the issue. The ability to compromise is an integral characteristic of the emotionally and spiritually mature person (see Acts 15:1-29). While we don't want our feelings to be ignored and trampled underfoot, neither do we want to do the same to the other person. It is characteristic of the immature person to either demand his way or to perpetually give in. In *Caring Enough to Confront*, David Augsburger writes (pages 8,13):

> Compromise is a gift to human relationships. We move forward on the basis of thoughtful, careful consensus and compromise in most decisions in conflict. But it

calls for at least a partial sacrifice of deeply held views and goals . . . to reach . . . agreement . . . Working through differences by giving clear messages of "I care" and "I want," which both care and confront, is most helpful.

This is interpersonal communication at its best. Caring—I want to stay in respectful relationships with you, and I want you to know where I stand and what I am feeling, needing, valuing and wanting.

. . . These are the two arms of genuine relationship: confrontation with truth; affirmation with love.

### Pass Over the Issue

At times we must learn to pass over the issue. This is not repression, which is denying the existence of a significant problem and burying any accompanying feelings. Though it is somewhat similar to withdrawing, the internal feelings and the basis are different. The basis for passing over the issue is realizing that the best possible solution to the problem, both for ourselves and for the other person, is to simply drop the issue. It means that we *hold no grudges,* that we are *willing to forgive and forget.*

*Caring Enough to Confront* puts it this way (page ii): "I am responsible for the way I react to you. You cannot make me angry unless I choose to be angry. You cannot make me discouraged, or disgusted, or depressed." Within certain limits it is true that we can choose not to get angry. In his book titled *In Two Minds,* Os Guinness also makes this point (page 207): "The key is to realize that no one is primarily responsible to God for what other people *have done* to him, whether through actions or teaching; the other people are responsible to God for this. But each person is responsible to God for what he has *done with* what others have done to him."

Passing over an issue involves a *full awareness* of the injury done to us and a deliberate willingness to *completely* drop the charges against the person(s) who has hurt us. We may decide that we don't have a good enough case or that it's not worth the expense to us and the other person to press charges.

For example, I have found that I can choose whether to react with or without anger to a scratch or dent somebody made in my car. Sure, I don't like scratches on my car, but I also realize that a car is only a material possession and often is not worth the emotional trauma. That doesn't mean that I would never take the name of the party at fault and try to get him to pay for the damages. It merely means that there are times when I may choose to pass over the anger-producing problem. I am also finding that as I become more mature I am able to pass over more conflicts.

The other night as I started to back out of the parking lot at work, I noticed that one headlight wasn't working. I got out of the car to see why and discovered that it was smashed. The car parked in front of me had a high bumper that could easily have smashed the headlight when squeezing into the tight spot in front of me. But when I thought about what a hassle it would be to try to find the owner and to confront him as to whether his car broke my headlight, with all the ensuing emotional turmoil, I chose to drop the issue. I drove home and the next day paid $1.59 to replace the light. That was a bargain in comparison to the time and conflict it might otherwise have cost.

Several years ago we bought a toilet seat from a large department store. It was guaranteed in writing never to break. There was just one problem—it kept breaking. Several times we've gone back to have the parts replaced, but it's always a struggle to get the store to honor its guarantee. Though there is no question in our minds that we are right in trying to replace the part, it's just not worth the emotional price tag to fight them, and so we've decided to pass over the issue and let the matter drop.

I've worked in county hospitals and have seen much that I don't like. On some things I've taken a stand, but on other issues I've decided that for me, it isn't worth the price involved to take a stand even though injustices are done. I must decide on what issues I will take a stand. On some I should take a stand. This topic will be discussed under the heading "Stand for Righteous Principles" in Chapter 10. But I will become a critical, negative, and hostile person if I start fighting every issue.

We must choose our battles. The world is filled with injustices and irritants. Jesus chose to deal with the Pharisees at certain times, but He also passed over many other issues that He legitimately could have fought. For example, slavery was common in those days, but He chose not to deal with that issue. Also, the country was occupied by Roman soldiers at that time, which was probably an unfair situation, but He didn't deal with that issue either.

Proverbs 19:11 says, "The discretion of a man deferreth his anger, and it is his glory to pass over a transgression" (KVJ). First Peter 2:23 points out that Jesus could accept unjust treatment and let it pass because He knew that God would someday judge the entire situation righteously and would take action against the person who had wronged Him.

# Chapter

# Seven

## *How to Forgive and Forget*

The final step in dealing with anger, and perhaps the most crucial one, is to forgive and forget. Matthew 6:15 warns, "But if you do not forgive others their trespasses—their reckless and willful sins, leaving them, letting them go and giving up resentment—neither will your Father forgive your trespasses" (AMP).

Often people have misconceptions about what forgiveness really is. Many of us, when trying to forgive someone, try to talk ourselves into thinking that what the other person did wasn't really wrong, or that he didn't really mean to do it, or that we over-reacted to what he did. This may sometimes be the case, but at other times we need to fully recognize that what the other person did was definitely wrong, but that we will nevertheless forgive him and forget it, no matter how much he has hurt us.

Forgiving means that we actively choose to give up our grudge despite the severity of the injustice done to us. It does not mean that we have to say or feel "That didn't hurt me" or "It didn't really matter." Some things may hurt very much, and we must not deny that fact, but after fully recognizing the hurt, we should choose to forgive.

Secondly, forgiving doesn't mean that the party at fault doesn't need to suffer the natural or lawful consequences of his actions. One can forgive and still allow justice to be administered. For example, if a drunken driver kills your child while driving recklessly, it is appropriate that legal action be taken against him. This is necessary not only for your child's sake, but also for the driver's and society's sake.

To bring this a little closer to home, let's say that your child is aware that you are angry at him for something he has done. He admits he was wrong and asks your forgiveness. If he is sincere, I believe it is your responsibility to forgive him. This doesn't mean that you don't have to discipline him, but it does mean that after you have discussed the problem with him and both of you have had the opportunity to share your feelings, you should give up your feelings of anger toward him.

Very often we come to this step of forgiving and forgetting after we have taken some of the previous steps for dealing with anger. No matter how many steps we have already taken, if we don't forgive the person and try to forget the situation, there are going to be repercussions in our own lives. Somehow we have the distorted notion that the other person suffers when we hold a grudge against him. Usually this is not the case. When you hold a grudge, often the other person doesn't even know about it, and even if he does, he probably doesn't care.

The only person who is being hurt is you. Holding a grudge and refusing to forgive is like licking our emotional wounds, which we all instinctively enjoy, but what we must realize is that we suffer greatly because of the weight of that grudge which we hold.

This is true even if we haven't consciously thought about the matter for a long time. If the problem is buried in our subconscious or unconscious mind, so that we aren't even aware of it, it's still constantly extracting something from us emotionally. And no one else can be blamed for that part of the emotional weight; we have put it upon ourselves.

There is a spiritual law given in Matthew 6:15 that says that when we do not forgive others, we ourselves sit and labor under the feeling of guilt and the load of the wrong that we are holding against another person. More will be said about this subject in Chapter 10.

### Handling Anger Destructively

Illustration 5-a shows the four paths which people commonly take when angry (which have been previously discussed). Unfortunately, these are basically destructive reactions. On the left-hand side of the illustration is the initial hurt or insult and the resulting feeling of anger. The first method listed is to attack, which could perhaps be better described as a hostile counterattack. While this releases a lot of internal pressure in the hurt person, it creates tremendous emotional conflicts between the people involved, often without resolving the original problem. The second commonly used method is to run from the problem. This is where the person refuses to talk about the problem or physically leaves the person or situation without really resolving his feelings, and so ends up holding a grudge.

The third approach is to give in. Here the person doesn't run from the situation, but externally submits to it. However, he doesn't

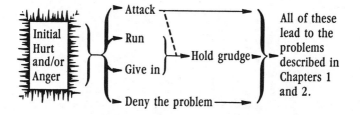

**Illustration 5-a**
**Handling Anger Destructively**

resolve the conflict internally, and thus adds to his unresolved anger fund. The fourth destructive reaction is to totally deny the hurt and the angry feelings. This person doesn't hold a grudge at a conscious level, but the problem is buried in his unconscious mind and causes internal disturbances. These four reactions are the usual ways that people handle anger, but they only add to the person's problems, even though the emotional and physical symptoms may not be apparent for years.

## Handling Anger Constructively

The diagram on page 131 (Illustration 5-b) summarizes the steps for handling anger constructively that have been described in

| STEP #1 | STEP #2 | STEP #3 | STEP #4 | STEP #5 | STEP #6 | STEP #7 |
|---------|---------|---------|---------|---------|---------|---------|
| Recognize your feelings and evaluate how upset you are. | Suppress taking action until you have thought through the situation and have full control of your words and actions. | Pray or have a prayerful attitude. This step is appropriate anywhere in the sequence. | Identify the true cause of your anger. | Evaluate whether your anger has a legitimate basis. | 1. Confront and inform. Share "I feel" message. Rebuke in love. <br> 2. Establish limits with consequences. <br> 3. Get counsel. <br> 4. Catharsis. <br> 5. Compromise. <br> 6. Pass over the issue. | Forgive and forget. | Resolution of hurt and anger. |

Initial Hurt and/or Anger

**Illustration 5-b**
**Handling Anger Constructively**

this chapter and the previous chapter. On the left side of the page we have the initial hurt or anger. Moving to the right on the diagram, the first step is to recognize those hurt or angry feelings and to evaluate how strong they are. The second step is to suppress taking any action until you have thought through the problem adequately and are sure you have full control of your words and actions.

I have listed Step 3 as praying or just having a prayerful attitude, one of "Lord, help me." It almost goes without saying that it is appropriate to stop and pray at any point in the proceedings. Thus this step has been enclosed in brackets to indicate that it is optional and can be used at any step in the sequence.

The fourth step is to identify the reason for your anger, to find out what is really upsetting you, to find the root cause of the problem. The fifth step is to evaluate whether your anger has a legitimate basis; that is, are the person's criticisms or actions valid, or are they unjustified? If you do have a legitimate cause for your anger, then you have to decide on one of the appropriate courses of action outlined in Step 6.

The various options in Step 6 are confrontation, establishing limits of behavior with consequences, getting counsel, undergoing catharsis, compromising, or passing over the issue. A combination of these courses of action is also possible. For example, you might get some counseling, then confront the individual, and then compromise. When Step 6 is completed, you *must* move on to Step 7, which is forgiving and forgetting. This should lead naturally to the resolution of your hurt or angry feelings and often the resolution of the external problem causing your feelings.

You might note which of these two approaches is more difficult: the one outlined in Illustration 5-a or the one outlined in Illustration 5-b. Obviously, handling and using anger constructively is a more complicated and drawn-out procedure. It takes more time, effort, and skill than handling anger destructively. However, once you have learned the skills, it takes much less time and effort to resolve conflict than when first learning these skills.

It's like learning to drive a car or learning a foreign language. It's always hard work at first and you make a lot of mistakes, but eventually it becomes second nature—you hardly need to think about it. The same thing happens in handling anger. As time goes on, you become more adept at handling situations in the different appropriate ways with less effort and with much-more-effective resolutions.

In addition, it is important to point out that each of these steps or skills will be necessary to use at one time or another. The particular means you choose will depend on the given situation and your ability to think through and select the best course of action. We must be familiar with and able to use each of these skills or we will run into difficulty. Not being able to draw on a particular skill when it is needed is a gigantic handicap.

## *Summary*

This entire process of handling anger constructively in these strained moments when you are emotionally upset can be summed up with the following two passages, one from the Old Testament and one from the New Testament. Leviticus 19:17,18 says, "Don't hate your brother. Rebuke anyone who sins; don't let him get away with it, or you will be equally guilty. Don't seek vengeance. Don't bear a grudge, but love your neighbor as yourself, for I am Jehovah" (TLB).

I've quoted Ephesians 4:25-32 often; nevertheless, I feel that its message bears repeating. It tells us to speak the truth honestly to each other; it encourages us to get angry appropriately; it warns us not to hold a grudge; it urges us to strive to forgive each other, to be "kind to one another, tenderhearted, forgiving one another, as God in Christ forgave you" (RSV).

# Chapter

# Eight

## *Practice What You Know*

### *The "Numb" Person*

Remember Jan, the coed who was ready to jump off the Vincent Thomas Bridge in San Pedro? How does someone as numb to feelings as Jan was apply the principles we have been describing? This plight could be compared to the glowing embers of a fire that are almost extinguished—you gently fan or blow on them to get them to glow a little brighter, hoping that eventually the fire will "catch."

People like Jan need help in getting in touch with those faint feelings that are barely perceptible. They may be feelings of hurt, irritation, annoyance, or anger. Any feeling or description close to this will do. However, the ideas presented in the previous pages may be so threatening that at first I don't particularly want people to *do* anything about the feelings; I just want them to be aware of the slightest twinge—that's all for now.

Often I will ask such people to list five things that cause them some negative feelings during the next week, and then to bring the list to their next session. This assignment may be repeated during a number of weeks, until the people become more familiar and comfortable in looking for these irritants that are in their life, but that they have learned to bury.

When they become proficient in this step, the next week I have them grade the items that occur, from a scale of one to ten. One stands for a very minimal hurt or displeasure and ten for a maximal discomfort. This is repeated as many weeks as is necessary until the person becomes sensitive to his feelings.

This completes Step No. 1 of chapter seven, the major deficit in the "numb" person.

### The Overwhelmed Person

I think of a woman with whom I was working who initially denied any problem with anger. After a few weeks of listing her hurts she became amazed at how many things really did bother her. She then went to the other extreme of noting so many things that bothered her that she was overwhelmed with what to deal with. I commended her for the excellent job she had done in getting in touch with her feelings. She was encouraged to pick at least one item that created a lot of displeasure, and then concentrate on applying the principles outlined in the previous chapter to constructively resolve that one problem. She could take a second or third item on a given week if she wanted to, but that was optional. If an item was too threatening or overwhelming to work on, an easier one could be substituted. The next week she was to repeat this, working on a couple of major items and letting the rest go.

She was amazed to find that within a month several phenomenal things occurred. First, her suicidal depression was gone. Second, her feelings of worth skyrocketed, and third, her previously overwhelming lists of hurts, irritations, and items of anger had greatly decreased. Lastly, her relationships with people improved markedly.

### The Mismatched Couple

How do you help a couple in which one partner is extremely proficient in the skills I have been emphasizing and the other is not? This frequently occurs in my practice. Contrary to what some might expect, it seems to

me that a greater percentage of my male patients have difficulty in this area than female
patients.

When I see a couple like this I try to convey to them the idea that both individuals
play a significant role in improving the situation. I liken it to a heavyweight boxer getting
into the ring and teaching a novice bantam-
weight how to fight. This will never be
achieved unless the heavyweight deliberately restrains himself. Thus the partner
who is more proficient in handling feelings
and confronting must tone down his side of
any conflict, especially avoiding any aggres-
siveness. Also, there must be tremendous
sensitivity to the feelings of the one who is
having the greater difficulty. There must be
the awareness that if the more capable
spouse keeps winning all the battles, both
parties will ultimately lose. As the stronger
one backs off and the other partner works on
getting in touch and expressing his or her
feelings, both will gain in the long run. If the
couple is not able to do this on their own,
they may need a therapist to facilitate
this process.

Though I see this problem most often in
married couples, it does occur in other situations. In those circumstances the process of
helping is usually complicated by the fact
that the more competent person won't easily

back off, so that we are left with the alternative of professionally assisting the one struggling with these skills.

### I Don't Want To Hurt Them

Collene, a sensitive minister's wife, has been learning the principles of the preceding chapters. She now is in touch with feelings buried for years. Last week she was all set to start sharing some of her feelings with relatives and parishioners who have been taking her for granted for years. But she returned to the office this week stating that she couldn't share her feelings or confront anyone because she "didn't want to hurt anyone."

This is a frequent obstacle. Often its roots go to the early years in the person's life and the type of instruction received, especially from parents. Also, this person is often very sensitive, especially regarding the way the confrontations might affect other people. Often when someone like Collene expresses her feelings it seems so strong, harsh, and uncomfortable to her, even though the other person hardly notices it. All of this awareness can help very sensitive people have more courage to share their feelings, but ultimately they must just *do* it, realizing the tremendous consequences if they don't. With practice it becomes much easier.

Finally, individuals like Collene must be willing to risk their "nice" or "she-is-always-so-sweet" label if they want to avoid the predictable consequences of buried hurts and anger described in the first two chapters of this book.

### *I Didn't Handle the Conflict Constructively*

Sue mustered up enough courage to confront her neighbor about her repeatedly using Sue as a babysitter. Sue had rehearsed in her mind how she would "constructively" approach her neighbor about the issue. Yesterday the neighbor brought her unruly two-year-old and simply stated, "I'll be back in two or three hours to pick up Terry." A surge of anger overwhelmed Sue and she blurted out, "You're always doing this—it makes me so angry."

Today Sue sits in my office feeling very "down" and "guilty" for sending such a strong, attacking message to her best friend, and she is retreating to her previous ways of burying all feelings. Certainly she doesn't want to become an angry, attacking person.

I had empathy for Sue's feelings and expressed my own understanding as to why she felt depressed and had retreated. But I didn't stop there—I commended her for trying to apply these principles. It may be that she didn't apply them in the most ideal way, but for her this was a real step of progress. With continued *practice* she would perfect these skills, and in the meantime she needed to be satisfied with her honest efforts at correcting this area of her life.

### Fear of Put-Downs

One of the commonly expressed fears people have about confronting others or sending "I feel" messages is that they will either be laughed at or ignored. If you send an "I feel" message and someone laughs at you, I would suggest sending a second "I feel" message which expresses your feelings about being laughed at. Thus you might have to send two or more messages in succession before being heard.

A few years ago in an adolescent psychotherapy group, a 16-year-old girl told how her mother used to go into her bedroom without knocking and search her drawers and personal items when she was at school. This girl told the group that she shared her "I feel" messages once, twice, and three times without apparent success, but she kept on sending them. She reported that only after the twenty-seventh time did her mother get the message and change her behavior—but then it worked!

## When to Use These Principles

A question that frequently arises when a person applies these principles is: "How do I know if an issue should be dealt with according to the steps in the previous chapter?" This is an excellent question, and answering it involves a number of complex issues. Generally I advise that any issue or problem that is apt to keep crossing your mind with some feelings of hurt, irritation, or anger, especially for a day or more after the initial feelings of displeasure were noted, should be submitted to the steps previously outlined. With the consistent application of these principles in your life (not avoiding them because they are hard), you will soon learn to recognize those issues which can be immediately passed over and those which require other action.

Another frequently asked question is: "How do I know if I have to confront the person about the issues?" If there is any question about the legitimacy of the issue, or if expectations are not clearly understood, the odds are high that you need to talk it over with the other person. Also, if you have trouble in forgiving and forgetting or in passing over the issue, and if catharsis doesn't seem to resolve the problem, the odds are high that you need to talk it over with the party involved, especially if you have not previously attempted to do so with that person and that issue.

These examples and comments are all generalizations to help you get started. With practice, with a willingness to do whatever you should, and with a sensitivity to God to direct you in this crucial area of your life, you will gain expertise and greater ease in properly handling your hurts, irritations, and anger.

# Chapter

# Nine

## *Preventing Anger*

If you want to be emotionally mature and able to handle anger when it arises, then there is work that needs to be done in the intervening hours or days when you aren't angry. Your unresolved anger fund needs to be reduced of any balance that may have accumulated over your lifetime. Also, there are a number of other things that must be done and a number of areas of your life that must be reevaluated so that you will respond maturely to conflict situations. Dealing with anger in the quiet periods when you're not angry decreases the frequency, the intensity, and the inappropriateness of your anger.

## Maintain a Purposeful Life

Good health habits are essential in minimizing anger. When we are tired we are much more prone to snap at others and to overreact to small irritants. Our tolerance for pressures and new problems is definitely lowered. Proper diet, rest, relaxation, and exercise are essential. Other miscellaneous items, such as keeping down excessive noise and clutter in our backgrounds, should also be considered. (See 1 Thessalonians 4:11 and Ecclesiastes 9:17.)

In addition to maintaining a physically active life, it is essential to maintain an active life in general. People who have positive pursuits in their lives have less time and reason to be angry than people who are stuck in a rut. The person who is progressing toward personal goals is less likely to be jealous of another person's success, which often manifests itself in anger. Thus, if you don't have meaningful, constructive goals for both your work and your leisure hours, this is something you need to correct.

## Have a Proper Relationship with God

It is my conviction that a right relationship with God is a tremendous aid in giving one a proper perspective on all the issues that we have been talking about. This relationship with God also eliminates the animosity that often exists between ourselves and others. When we begin to realize all that God has done for us despite the hurts we have inflicted on others, it can't help but soften our tendency to be angry at others for the hurts that they have inflicted on us. In addition, periodic time alone with God, reading the Bible, praying, and meditating can help clarify areas in our lives that need working on and can better prepare us to handle conflict as it arises.

A compromised Christian life undoubtedly makes a person more prone to anger. The example of Balaam illustrates this (see Numbers 22:26-33). God allowed Balaam's donkey to irritate Balaam, which caused Balaam to pause in his wrongdoing to get angry at his donkey. Balaam failed to see that the hand of God was behind this irritation, trying to warn him. Thus when God needs to, in His permissive will, He uses disappointments, hurts, and suffering to get our attention. If we don't get the message, we may end up just getting angry. Job 36:18 says, "Don't let your anger at others lead you into scoffing at God! Don't let your suffering embitter you at the only one who can deliver you'' (TLB). (See *Living God's Will,* by the author.)

### *Evaluate Your Rights and Expectations*

Some people teach that we have no rights, that we should live to serve others and be willing to do whatever others ask of us, never thinking of our own desires or needs. They cite the passage in the Sermon on the Mount (Matthew 5) that tells us that if someone strikes us on the right cheek, we should offer the other cheek; that if someone asks us for our coat, we should give him our shirt also; that if someone forces us to walk a mile with him, we should go the second mile. They see the Christian life as one of total submission, in which we take whatever comes our way and never offer any resistance. The implication of this teaching in terms of anger is that if we expect nothing from life or from others, we will not be disappointed and angry when we suffer misfortunes.

I believe it's normal to have certain rights and expectations. In fact, I would go so far as to say that if we really lived as if we had absolutely no rights we would be poor stewards of all that God has given us and would probably die in a short time. There are always people who have greater needs than ours, and if we believe we have no rights, we will give away everything we have and every shred of ourselves to these people who are more needy than we are. I agree that if we really believe we have no rights and do not have any expectations, much of our anger problem can be resolved. However, dealing with the entire problem of anger in this way is, in my opinion, very naive.

On the other hand, there is no question that inappropriate rights and expectations are a major cause of problems for many people. People get angry if what they conclude to be their rights are not satisfied or if their expectations are not met. Very often these "rights" and expectations have never been fully put into words; in fact, they are sometimes subconscious or even unconscious in nature. And if those expectations were put into words, the person might be embarrassed or even deny them.

The more rights and expectations we have, whether we are aware of them or not, the more things we have to get angry about. I have seen people in therapy who believe that it is their right not to work and that society should take care of their needs, even though they are young and healthy. They would never admit this in so many words, but when you really get to know them it is clear that this is their expectation.

At present I can think of several people who are angry over the fact that they have had to start at the bottom of the company and work up to the top. Or there is the husband who has concluded that it is his exclusive right to decide if his marriage is to remain intact. Now these may seem to be extreme examples, but I can also cite thousands more that may seem minor in comparison but still create havoc in interpersonal relationships every day.

Every time you get hurt, angry, frustrated, or disappointed, some contract that you hold onto is being violated. You may quickly protest, "I haven't entered into any contracts! What do you mean, some contract is being violated?" Let me illustrate.

Every person entering into a close relationship, whether at home, at work, or within any group where people are working closely together, has at least three levels of expectations. At the first level are the *expressed expectations*. These are the expectations that are clearly defined between you and the other person. These may be written down but are most often verbalized.

At another level are the *unexpressed but conscious expectations*. These expectations are those that have been consciously concluded in one's own mind, but which have never been expressed verbally. The reasons for this could be that the person fears the disapproval of others or that it is difficult for the person to express his feelings. The expectations may not even be clearly enough defined in the person's mind to be expressed in words. Nevertheless, they are there. Our expectations still don't stop at this level. There is one deeper level, the *unconscious expectations*, which are not clearly defined even to oneself.

So you can see that each person entering into a close relationship, especially marriage, has three levels of expectations. This gives much opportunity for hurt, irritation, or anger to develop. (This theme of hidden expectations is described more fully in *Marriage Contracts and Couple Therapy*, by Clifford J. Segar, M.D.)

There is a game that is often played in close relationships that I've called "The Hidden Test of Expectancy." It goes like this: The button is missing from my brown suit. I know my wife is aware of this because she happened to notice that it was off a week ago, the last time I wore the suit. I know she is busy, but a week has gone by and the button is still missing. I reason that *if she really loves me* she would know that I want to wear that suit and would have mended it without my having to bring it to her attention. In fact, I muse, I'll see just how much she loves me by seeing how long it takes her to mend it.

Another week passes, and one day she comments that I seem to be wearing my sport coat more frequently lately. I casually reply, "Well, I haven't worn it for a long time so I thought I'd get a little wear out of it." However, as I drive to work I realize that I'm quite irritated because she has failed my test of expectancy by not sewing on the button yet.

It's not difficult to see how destructive this sort of game is, and I believe that if we really care about a relationship we need to stop such games. When something is important to us, our *feelings and desires* should be shared with those of whom we have the expectations. *Caring Enough to Confront* says (page 24), "Keep short books with your feelings. Stay up to date. Find ways of reporting feelings as they occur. Experiment in saying both what you feel and what you really want."

How can a person determine if he has a lot of concluded rights and expectations? Often the best way is to list all the things that tend to upset you, irritate you, or make you angry. By taking a good hard look at each item on that list, you can usually figure out what you have concluded to be your rights, whether legitimate ones or more questionable ones.

There is no question in my mind that one of the quickest ways to change hurt and angry feelings is to look at your expectations and change those that are inappropriate or unrealistic. As those rights and expectations are changed, both the primary feelings of being hurt and the secondary feelings of anger that may result will dissolve. On the other hand, if you don't deal with the inappropriate expectations you will continue to react with anger as if those expectations were in fact valid. Reacting with hurt and anger, or even confronting the other person in this situation, only tends to aggravate the problem.

I'm afraid that all too frequently we are afraid to be honest with ourselves about our expectations. Often we are embarrassed to verbalize them even to ourselves, let alone to others. Nevertheless, our unconscious minds act on the basis of those hidden expectations even though we are not fully aware of them. Thus it is crucial that we get in touch with all our "rights" and expectations.

### Express Your Expectations

Once we have gotten in touch with all our demands and expectations and have admitted them to ourselves, we need to express them to those we have the expectations of. That is the only way to have a truly honest, open relationship. Otherwise it's like two people playing a game when only one of them knows all the rules. We need their feedback as to whether our expectations are valid and mutually agreed upon. Those that aren't mutually agreed upon must be negotiated, or else trouble will be inevitable. In addition to expressing our expectations, we must also express our needs, and at times our wishes and desires. In close relationships, like those at home, work, or church, so much hurt comes from failing to share and discuss these matters.

Many of us who want to be "nice" people cringe at the thought of expressing expectations. Somehow it doesn't seem that a loving person should do something as crass as this. However, I would suggest that withholding your desires creates more havoc than tactfully and honestly expressing them when the need arises.

I've seen several Christians accept so-called "full-time" Christian jobs. When they entered into the negotiations about the salary, benefits, and responsibilities of the job, they portrayed a "loving" and "anything's okay" attitude. But I have had the opportunity to keep in contact with some of these people for a number of years and have observed their nonverbalized and possibly unrealized expectations. When those expectations weren't met they were hurt, and sometimes even bitter and angry. How much better it would have been for all parties involved if they had initially formulated their expectations in their own minds and then expressed them, rather than undergoing all the ill feelings that inevitably resulted.

Expressing expectations and at times actually coming to a contractual agreement can save a lot of time, money, and emotional energy. Abimelech and his men used and took possession of an important well that belonged to Abraham. Abraham prudently gave Abimelech a gift, and then in a sense he extracted a covenant or agreement stating that the well was in fact Abraham's (Genesis 21:25-32).

In my last year of residency in psychiatry I was allowed a certain amount of elective time to pursue special interests. I wanted to sharpen my skills in one particular area, but I had heard that this department tended to make increasing demands on one's time and energy. I had observed some of the problems that this created for other residents. At first my choices seemed to be to either avoid this area altogether, which would have been to my loss, or else to allow myself to get involved, knowing that eventually I would become frustrated and angry when increasing demands were placed upon my already-busy schedule.

I didn't like either of these options, so I did something that, to my knowledge, no one had ever done before in this department. I wrote a proposal which stated exactly what I wanted to do in that elective, the amount of time that I would be willing to give, and also my expectations from the people involved. Furthermore, I listed a number of things that I did not want to occur. Then I submitted this to all the parties involved. Obviously, they had a free choice as to whether to accept my proposal, and whether to make any changes or to reject it. As it turned out, they accepted it exactly as proposed.

Shortly thereafter my superior kidded me, "Did you have a lawyer brother draft that contract?" I told him that I hadn't, but that I wanted to draft it for the sake of all involved and because of what I had observed in my colleagues in previous years. Despite this explanation, this same individual put pressure on me three times to do more and more "for my education." It was a great relief to me to remind him of our mutual agreement and to suggest that we look at it together in case either of us had forgotten the items covered. He said, "No, that won't be necessary," and the pressures were removed.

If I had not drawn up that agreement I probably would have been furious and had a difficult time resolving the conflict. However, with the contract I was only slightly annoyed but was able to "pass over" the issue fairly easily without having it damage my relationship with the department or this individual. Clearly delineating one's expectations, and perhaps even expressing them in the form of a contract, can prevent a lot of angry situations.

As discussed in Chapter 6, for people in positions of authority, it can be crucial that not only expectations in the form of limit-setting be done, but also that the consequences for exceeding those limits be predetermined. This has a tremendous preventive effect in dealing with anger in one's life.

### Be Realistic in Self-Expectations

Sometimes we expect too much of ourselves. We don't take into account, or we refuse to admit, that we are human and thus have certain limitations. I have worked with patients who expect an A average in college or graduate school, some who demand that their house always be immaculate, and others who need to look like a model every time they are seen by another human being. This problem can express itself in the form of overextending ourselves, trying to cram too much into one day. Then, when we can't accomplish what we set out to do, we become angry at ourselves or at whatever interferes with our schedule.

Sometimes we have a need to please others, and when their expectations become difficult or impossible to meet, we become angry at them or at ourselves. Often this problem has its roots in feelings of inadequacy and insecurity, a subject which we will touch upon later.

### Expect the Right Things from God

I believe that every person in this universe has expectations of God, regardless of his belief about the existence of God. One person might say, "If God exists, He should be good and remove all evil and suffering from the earth." Another person may retort, "If there is a God, He should reveal Himself to me in a way that will not require faith on my part." Many people feel that they shouldn't have to suffer through difficulties or problems, whether physical, emotional, or financial. It's as though God owes them a comfortable life.

These expectations are seldom consciously thought through or verbalized, but they are nevertheless at work in daily life. To see this most vividly, observe the reactions of the person who has lost a job, has had a financial reversal, is confronted with a serious illness, or has lost a loved one. The reaction that follows the thwarting of an expectation from God can often take the form of anger, resentment, bitterness, and depression.

What do we do if we find ourselves reacting in this way to our unmet expectations? Whether they are appropriate or inappropriate, we need to be honest about all those feelings, for it certainly is much better to be honest than to deny their existence. This honesty with our feelings is healthy for several reasons.

As these expectations are put out in the open with God, this puts things up front in our relationship with God and allows the issues to become clearer, so that they can be dealt with more effectively.

Will God get angry if I express my honest feelings to Him? The books of Psalms and Job are full of feelings of disappointment, misunderstanding, and anger at God. Jeremiah, Habakkuk, Job, and David all vented their hurt and upset feelings, and probably because of this were able to work through the difficult situations in which they found themselves. However, it is worthy to note that in venting our feelings and airing our doubts, questions, or fears to God—who already knows all about them—we must be careful not to curse God in the process (see Job 1:22).

Another reason that it is healthy to be honest about our feelings is that as we are honest about our expectations we are in a better position to sort out the appropriate ones from the inappropriate ones. For some illustrations of inappropriate expectations in the Scriptures, see the accounts of Kings Ahab and Uzziah, who both became very angry when their wishes were not met (1 Kings 21 and 2 Chronicles 26:16-20). Another example is the faithful, older brother who became angry when the younger, prodigal son was honored at a party (Luke 15). In each case expectations were not met and anger was the result.

Being honest with God often leads to another interesting development. As we are honest with God and ourselves, we often become aware of excessive expectations that we are placing on ourselves. God would like to liberate us from these. While God has promised the *believer* eternal life, guidance, peace, and scores of other blessings that He wants us to claim, we must be careful that we apply His promises properly and meet the conditions required. Also, we need to keep in mind that all the promises are not blanket statements to everyone.

Job, although he was the most righteous man on the face of the earth at that time, had to give up his health, his prosperity, his family, and even his good favor with his peers. This wasn't because he violated God's laws; it was because God had the right to allow those things to be taken from him. I realize that this may seem like an extreme example and unrelated to life as many of us experience it today. However, as we look around we see those who do suffer to this degree throughout the world.

It might seem that I've come full circle from where I started this section. I first said that we are all entitled to certain rights and expectations, and that it is unrealistic to live as though we had none at all. Now I seem to be saying that we should give them up.

My position is this: We all have many expectations, and attempting to remove them all, especially at once, is ill-advised and virtually impossible. However, we must continually be aware of what our expectations are, evaluating whether they are appropriate. If they are inappropriate, we must be willing to give them up. We must be willing to give up any expectation that God desires to change.

But let me hasten to make one more point. Sometimes after we have yielded something to God, He later restores it, even giving more in return. Naaman wanted a pompous ceremony to cure his leprosy, but he had to give up that demand. When he followed the more humbling procedure of bathing in the muddy Jordan River, he was completely cured (2 Kings 5). Job surrendered his "rights" and later received back twice as much as he had enjoyed previously. As soon as these people were willing to yield their rights, God returned abundantly more back to them.

### Accept the Facts of Life

A lot of things in life don't seem to be fair. If we take an honest look around us, it becomes clear that the person who has a high I.Q., money, good looks, good health, an attractive personality, and ample abilities and opportunities may have done nothing to get all these qualities.

On the other extreme is the person with an average or low I.Q. and none of the abilities or traits listed above. You and I are most likely somewhere between these two extremes. The parable of the talents in Matthew 25:15 says, "And to one he gave five talents, to another, two, to another, one." Thus God acknowledges the fact that individuals have various abilities.

If we compare ourselves with other people we will surely seem to come out short. The Joneses will always appear to have something more than we do. Even the man who has everything tends to ignore all that he has, and instead focuses on what he doesn't have.

We need to see life more from God's perspective—that life is a gift. The years that we have are a gift. The degree of health, wealth, and wisdom we have are gifts. If we allow our eyes to focus enviously on comparisons with others, we will miss the many things that God has done, is doing, and will do for us. Accepting ourselves and our assets—God's gifts to us—is fundamental to overcoming anger.

### Deal with Feelings of Inferiority

In my opinion there is a direct correlation between our feelings of inadequacy or inferiority and the anger in our lives. The more inadequate or inferior we feel, the greater the likelihood that we are going to be angry. On the other hand, the better we feel about ourselves, the less reason we will have to be defensive, bitter, and jealous. Notice also that I say our *feelings* of inadequacy and inferiority, because often there is very little correlation between our *feelings* of inadequacy and our *actual* capabilities. If we *feel* inadequate and inferior, we will be on our guard for anything that threatens our feelings of self-worth, and so we protect ourselves with angry counterattacks.

Dealing in depth with feelings of inadequacy and inferiority is beyond the scope of this book. However, I devote a chapter to this subject in *How to Win Over Fatigue* (formerly entitled *Run and Not be Weary*). Also, I recommend *Hide or Seek,* by James Dobson, an excellent book on this subject.

### Avoid Aggravating Situations

"Do not associate with a man given to anger, or go with a hot-tempered man, lest you learn his ways, and find a snare for yourself'' (Proverbs 2:24,25). We need to be aware that certain people are more prone to get angry at others, and that some of this anger may rub off on us. Also, certain situations may be more anger-producing than others, and unless we have an unusually good reason for being around these people or situations, we should consider removing ourselves from such influences.

Sometimes we find ourselves in situations where it is difficult to resolve anger constructively. An example might be the unreasonable boss. In that situation we have to take a hard look at either changing ourselves or the relationship, and if neither of these is feasible, we may have to change jobs.

An unreasonable spouse is probably the most difficult situation in which we could find ourselves. Conscientiously and consistently applying the principles in this book can help tremendously, but where that is not enough, outside help, possibly professional, is necessary.

### *Reduce Your Unresolved Anger Fund*

The amount of energy that is tied up in hurt and anger is truly incalculable. At a moment's notice King Herod's stepdaughter, after being advised by her mother, Herodias, rejected an offer of up to half the kingdom, and instead chose to have John the Baptist beheaded. John had told King Herod that it wasn't lawful for him to be married to his brother's wife, Herodias. This angered Herodias, and so she "had a grudge against him and wanted to kill him, and could not do so" (Mark 6:19). Like Herodias, many of us have large reserves in our unresolved anger fund which are using up tremendous amounts of psychic energy.

The question now is, How do we get rid of this unresolved anger fund? How do we deplete it? I think we can get some clues if we consider how this fund developed in the first place. Every time there was a situation that left a hurt or frustration that was not handled constructively, it accumulated in our unresolved anger fund.

The charged emotions were pushed down inside. In order to get rid of this reserve in the anger fund, I believe we must go back and do the constructive work that was not done initially. This may seem to be a simplistic approach for dissipating destructive energy, but it is basically what must be done.

First, we must get in touch with the original feelings—the hurt, the pain, or the anger. The psychological term for the recall of repressed, painful memories and experiences is *abreaction*. Once a person has gotten in touch with his feelings, he then needs to handle them in a constructive way as outlined in the previous chapter. Thus, if he has repressed the hurt and anger, he really has only delayed doing the constructive work that must be done. But this person is paying a very high interest rate for every day he procrastinates in dealing constructively with that hurt or anger. Not only does he carry a tremendous weight during his lifetime, but he may also be unable to achieve his maximum potential.

Someone might ask, "When a person becomes a Christian, aren't old hurts in our lives removed? Aren't we the 'new creature' that 2 Corinthians 5:17 (KJV) talks about—'old things are passed away; behold, all things are become new'?" This is an excellent question, and I can only venture a reply. It is my opinion that when someone is converted, these things may or may not be resolved. That has nothing to do with whether the person is a Christian or is forgiven by God. If a person is born again he is a Christian and he is forgiven, but that doesn't necessarily mean that all the old hurts and wounds are automatically resolved.

Christ did not argue with Zacchaeus when he offered restitution for old offenses after his profession of faith (Luke 19; see also Matthew 5:23,24).

Let me illustrate this. First we have Mr. Smith. He is a 40-year-old man who has really lived a life of debauchery. But now he has hit bottom. He sees and gets in touch with his rotten self with its hurts, anger, and the like. He is aware of how phenomenal God's forgiveness is, and because he is in touch with his hurts, he forgives those who hurt him. He has satisfied the steps outlined in the previous chapter at the time of conversion. If he feels the need for restitution for some specific past deeds, he does so under the guidance of the Holy Spirit. Mr. Smith ends up walking on cloud nine emotionally and spiritually. He has cleaned out his unresolved anger fund. If from that day on he handles each new problem that develops constructively, he will not add to that potential fund. Mr. Smith not only became a Christian and experienced God's forgiveness, but he rid himself of tremendous amounts of unnecessary emotional baggage.

Now let's consider Mr. Jones. He led the same corrupt life as Mr. Smith, and at age 40 he realized that he needed to get right with God. But unlike Mr. Smith, he is only in touch with about half of his hurts, pain, and unresolved anger. He accepts Christ and feels cleansed, like a new person. His position before God is that of a forgiven man and he is a Christian, bound for heaven. But Mr. Jones has a moderate amount of unresolved hurts still residing within him. They may rear their ugly head from time to time, and he will find that conversion does not automatically resolve all emotional problems. He will need to get in touch with this unresolved anger fund and deal with it, possibly little by little. In addition, he will have to be careful that he doesn't accumulate new areas of unresolved anger which could quickly bring his fund back up to where it was before becoming a Christian.

Now let's look at Mr. Johnson. Mr. Johnson was raised in the church, and at the age of ten he accepted Christ and asked for forgiveness of his sins. At that age he was probably in touch with all of his areas of anger and hurt, and thus he cleaned out his anger account. However, in the ensuing years as he grew up in the church, he was hurt from time to time. If Mr. Johnson didn't learn how to deal with his hurts and anger, he could accumulate a large unresolved anger fund. Now, at age 40—the same age as Mr. Smith and Jones—though he has been a Christian for 30 years, he finds himself laboring under a tremendous weight, more than the other two men. He may even conclude that Christianity doesn't work.

If he wants to experience the abundant life, he will have to constructively resolve these hurts, possibly one at a time. He may even need professional help to do so. But if he doesn't in some way deal with them, the emotional weight will continue to take its toll.

I believe that this illustrates the relationship between our emotional hurts, our feelings, and our position before God. I believe that this view is consistent with the Scriptures, psychiatry, my observations of people around me, and my own life.

# Chapter

# Ten

## *Ideal Ways to Handle Anger*

Our ultimate goal should be to handle anger-producing situations in an extremely mature way—in a Christlike way. Christ was able to use all the constructive ways listed in previous chapters; however, He especially excelled in five areas: 1) His ability to stand up for righteous principles; 2) His ability to pass over inconsequential issues; 3) His ability to forgive; 4) His willingness to pray for those who hurt or misused him; 5) His ability to love, despite what was done against Him.

In my opinion, we should use the above five means which Christ demonstrated during His lifetime from a position of strength, not weakness. We must be able to do all

the things that have been listed earlier
to constructively resolve anger, and only
choose these more difficult means in some
situations.

This is what Christ actually did. Thus we
should never repress anger only to have it
crop up later in a more destructive way. For
example, I don't think you can pass over an
issue, forgive, or love if you aren't willing
and able to confront that individual.
Likewise, I don't believe you can really
stand for righteous principles unless you can
pass over an issue, forgive, and love.

A person must be emotionally and
spiritually mature to apply these more difficult means. He must feel good about
himself. He must genuinely care about the
relationship. He must feel secure and loved
by God. His deepest aim must be to please
God. If you found it difficult to use some of
the constructive means described earlier in
this book, I suggest that you work on those
first, before you work on these ideal
methods.

### *Stand for Righteous Principles*

Christian leaders down through centuries
have rephrased God's anger into "righteous

indignation." However, I think it is better to see that the emphasis is really on *standing for righteous principles.* Christ's entire life was given to this purpose, and at times while He was standing for these righteous principles, it became necessary for Him to express anger.

On occasion you will find a religious person who is angry, indignant, or self-seeking who cloaks it in an otherwise-good religious or moral enterprise. But this cloak doesn't change his anger into righteous indignation, nor does it mean that he is standing for righteous principles. God knows the true purpose of the heart, and if our motives aren't truly for Him, our righteous indignation is actually *selfish* indignation. Thus our activities and motives must be based on His will and a desire to stand for His principles.

The most prominent example of Christ's standing for righteous principles is when He threw the money changers out of the temple because they were misusing God's house (John 2:13-17). There were also other times that He expressed anger, especially towards the religious leaders of the day, whose legalism and hypocrisy hindered the common man from knowing God. In addition, many godly men throughout the Scriptures stood for righteous principles, as Moses,

Jonathan, Jeremiah, and Paul (see Exodus 19; 1 Samuel 19, 20; Jeremiah 6:11; Acts 13:9-11).

### Pass Over Inconsequential Issues

Christ had the ability to pass over inconsequential issues—that is, issues where no righteous principles were at stake. He could pass over issues which normally would hurt most people's pride. An excellent example of this is found in Mark 5, where the crowd laughed at Him because He said that Jairus' daughter was not dead but sleeping. Though He could easily have proven His point to the crowd once He had raised her from the dead, He left quietly and told the girl's parents to tell no one what had happened.

I have chosen to use the phrase "pass over inconsequential issues" because I think it helps clarify an important distinction. When we aren't very mature, a personal attack may be of major consequence to us, and there may be times when we will need to defend ourselves. However, as we feel better about ourselves, both emotionally and spiritually, there will be less need to defend ourselves because the issue will actually have become less important to us. In addition, as we are able to deal more constructively with the hurts and anger in our lives, our self-esteem will improve so that we will be able to pass over more issues. Proverbs 19:11 says, "A wise man restrains his anger and overlooks insults. This is to his credit" (TLB).

Eventually we will be in a position to choose to pass over more issues as they become more inconsequential to us. Again, we see that it is out of strength that we are able to pass over these things. Christ was sure of his position with God, and the more sure we are of our own position with Christ, the more inconsequential the issues will be.

But before this kind of emotional and spiritual maturity has taken place, we must be very careful about expecting ourselves or others to pass over issues which to them might be very important. I believe we have to be very careful about telling a five-year-old to "turn the other cheek." When other people hurt him, it is of major consequence to him. He may have to deal with it as most other five-year-olds do. Later, as he matures, he may be able to pass over such an issue.

### *Forgive*

Before we look at Jesus' ability and willingness to forgive, let's take a look at God's forgiveness toward us. There are two reasons for this: First, it is the ultimate example of the kind of forgiveness that we should aim for, and second, as we become aware of how much God has forgiven us, it truly tends to eclipse the injustices done against us for which we tend to be unforgiving.

God promises not only to forgive our sins, but to forget them, to the extent that He doesn't remember them anymore. Isaiah 38:17 says, "For thou hast cast all my sins behind thy back" (KJV). Isaiah 43:25 says, "I, even I, am the one who wipes out your transgressions for My own sake; and I will not remember your sins." The Living Bible renders this verse, "I, yes, I alone am he who blots away your sins for my own sake and will never think of them again." Hebrews 8:12 says, "For I will be merciful to their iniquities, and I will remember their sins no more." (See also Hebrews 10:17.)

Christ is our example of this kind of forgiveness. Though He was equal with God, He emptied himself of His rights and took upon Himself the status of a slave, and was obedient even to death (Philippians 2:5-8). Jesus took upon Himself the death penalty for our sins so that we could be forgiven. The Gospels record how He went to the cross without even defending Himself. The crowds made fun of Him, mocked Him, and humiliated Him; the soldiers stripped Him, beat Him, spit on Him, and finally hung Him on a cross to die a slow and painful death. What was His response to all of this? "Father, forgive them, for they know not what they are doing" (Luke 23:34).

You might say that these altruistic examples are great, but what about the rest of us? Stephen is a beautiful example of a man following Jesus' example (Acts 7). After he had shared the gospel with those around him, he was rejected along with the message he was trying to give. He knew he was right and they were wrong, but that wasn't the issue. Even while they were stoning him to death, he said, " 'Lord Jesus, receive my spirit!' And falling on his knees, he cried out with a loud voice, 'Lord, do not hold this sin against them!' " (Acts 7:59,60).

In Matthew 18 we are told to confront someone who has wronged us privately, and if that doesn't resolve the problem, we may have to involve others. However, immediately following this confrontation, we are told to forgive him. Peter once asked Christ how many times a man should forgive his brother—seven times? Jesus' answer was "seven times seventy" or 490 times, thus suggesting that our forgiveness should be limitless (Matthew 18:21,22).

Christ went on to illustrate this point by telling of a man who had a debt of ten million dollars who was forgiven this debt by the ruler of the land. But then this same man who had just been forgiven his debt viciously demanded payment from a very poor man who owed him only 20 dollars. When the king heard this, he told him, " 'You evil-hearted wretch! Here I forgave you all that tremendous debt, just because you asked me to—shouldn't you have mercy on others, just as I had mercy on you?' Then the angry king sent the man to the torture chamber until he had paid every last penny due. So shall my heavenly Father do to you if you refuse to truly forgive your brothers" (Matthew 18:32-34 TLB).

Thus when we become fully aware of the magnitude of our sins and God's priceless forgiveness to us, any wrongs that others have committed against us seem truly minor.

The Lord's Prayer also emphasizes this principle. It says in part, "Forgive us our sins, just as we have forgiven those who have sinned against us. Don't bring us into temptation, but deliver us from the Evil One. Amen.' Your heavenly Father will forgive you if you forgive those who sin against you; but if you refuse to forgive them, he will not forgive you" (Matthew 6:12-15 TLB; see also Mark 11:25).

Many of these principles are further exemplified in the books of 1 and 2 Corinthians. In 1 Corinthians 5, the church at Corinth was told to confront one of its members and take disciplinary action against him. Later,in 2 Corinthians, Paul wrote, "Now is the time to forgive him and comfort him. Otherwise he may become so bitter and discouraged that he won't be able to recover. Please show him now that you still do love him very much . . . A further reason for forgiveness is to keep from being outsmarted by Satan; for we know what he is trying to do" (2 Corinthians 2:7,8,11 TLB).

Forgiveness means giving up a right. It is like canceling a debt that someone owes you—it is costly. When we forgive we suffer a loss ourselves and we accept the fact that a loss has in fact occurred. If we don't forgive we are adamantly holding on to our "rights" and are continuing to demand recompense from the other person, even though it may be impossible for him to undo the wrong he has committed against us. Forgiveness is primarily a matter of the will. If we are harboring anger or hurt we are retaining our right or at least our wish for vengeance. As Archibald D. Hart says in *Feeling Free* (page

85): "Forgiveness is surrendering my right to hurt you back if you hurt me."

In addition, I believe that there is a relationship between how forgiven we feel and how readily we forgive others. When a person doesn't forgive others, often he labors under a lot of guilt and a feeling of not being fully forgiven himself, even though this guilt may be over other issues. It is almost a case of misery loving company—the person feels miserable and guilty, so why shouldn't someone else feel that way too?

Following the verse that has been quoted many times in this book—"Be angry and yet do not sin"—is the following admonition: "Let all bitterness and wrath and anger and clamor and slander be put away from you, along with all malice. And be kind to one another, tenderhearted, forgiving each other, just as God in Christ also has forgiven you" (Ephesians 4:31,32).

### Pray for the Offender

Christ not only was an example of One who could pass over issues, but He was even able to pray for those who crucified Him. On the cross, He prayed, "Father, forgive them, for they do not know what they are doing" (Luke 23:34).

Jesus tells us in Matthew 5:43,44, "You have heard that it was said, 'You shall love your neighbor and hate your enemy.' But I say to you, love your enemies and pray for those who persecute you." Thus we are commanded to love and to pray for those who have wronged us. It is difficult to hold a grudge against someone for whom we are praying sincerely.

Job's friends, though they intended to help him, actually hurt him and displeased God. Nevertheless, God required Job to pray for those friends. When he did, the friends received forgiveness and were reconciled to Job and to God. In addition, this act of praying for them opened the door so that God could restore all that had been taken from Job—in fact, twice as much as he had before.

### *Be Loving*

The very heart and essence of the Bible is God's willingness to love us despite all that we have done wrong. The Bible says, "God so loved the world" that He was able to give His most precious possession, His son. He was willing not only to forgive but to love. (See John 3:16.)

In 1 John 4:19 we read, "We love because He first loved us." Romans 12:17-21 says,

"Never pay back evil for evil to anyone . . . . If possible, so far as it depends on you, be at peace with all men. Never take your own revenge . . . but if your enemy is hungry, feed him, and if he is thirsty, give him a drink; for in so doing you will heap burning coals upon his head. Do not be overcome by evil, but overcome evil with good."

Thus Christ is our example of One who was willing to love even those who wronged Him, hurt Him, betrayed Him, deserted Him, beat Him, and even killed Him. As we comprehend His great love and forgiveness toward us, it will empower us to forgive and love those who hurt and wrong us in daily living.

# Bibliography

Augsburger, David. *Caring Enough to Confront*. Glendale: Regal Books, 1973.
This is an excellent book on confronting with love.

_____. *The Freedom of Forgiveness*. Chicago: Moody Press, 1970.

Bach, Dr. George R., and Goldberg, Dr. Herb. *Creative Aggression*. New York: Avon Books 1974.
This book overemphasizes, in my opinion, the role of being aggressive or expressing anger. Nevertheless, it makes some important points. The person who always wants to be "nice" and liked by all could profit from this if he keeps this fact in mind.

Carlson, Dwight L., M.D. *How to Win Over Fatigue* (formerly titled *Run and Not Be Weary*). Old Tappan, NJ: Fleming H. Revell Company, 1974.

_____. *Living God's Will*. Old Tappan, NJ: Fleming H. Revell Company, 1976.

Cooke, Joseph R. *Free for the Taking*. Old Tappan, NJ: Fleming H. Revell Company, 1975.
This is an excellent book for the very religious person who does not understand the proper role of feelings.

Dobson, James, Ph.D. *Hide or Seek*. Old Tappan, NJ: Fleming H. Revell Company, 1974.
An excellent book on self-esteem.

Ellis, Albert, Ph.D. *How to Live With and Without Anger.* New York: Readers Digest Press, 1977.

Gordon, Dr. Thomas. *Parent Effectiveness Training.* New York: Peter H. Wyden, Inc., Publisher, 1970.
This book and the P.E.T. classes that are offered in many communities have some strong and weak points. The strong points include teaching skills in empathic listening, getting in touch with feelings, and the idea that rigid authority is often not necessary.
It has several major weak areas. First, it holds the position that parental authority is never needed, and with this position I strongly disagree. Furthermore, the author plays down the role of parents instilling spiritual principles in the home. With this I also disagree. However, if a person can learn from the strengths in this book or in the classes and can ignore the weak points, the training may be very beneficial.

Jacobs, Joan. *Feelings.* Wheaton: Tyndale House, 1976.
An excellent book for individuals raised in religious legalism and rigidness.

Madow, Leo, M.D. *Anger.* New York: Charles Scribner's Sons, 1972.
An excellent secular book on anger.

Osborne, Cecil G. *The Art of Understanding Yourself.* Grand Rapids: Zondervan Books, 1967.

Powell, John S.J. *Why Am I Afraid to Tell You Who I Am?* Chicago: Argus Communications, 1969.

Rubin, Theodore Isaac, M.D. *The Angry Book*. London: The MacMillan Company, 1969.

Scoglund, Elizabeth R. *To Anger, With Love*. New York: Harper and Row, 1977.

Segar, Clifford J., M.D. *Marriage Contracts and Couple Therapy*. New York: Brunner/Mazel, Inc., 1976.

Viscott, David, M.D. *The Language of Feelings*. New York: Arbor House, 1976.

Wright, H. Norman. *Communication: Key to Your Marriage*. Glendale: Regal Books, 1974.

_____. *The Christian Use of Emotional Power*. Old Tappan, NJ: Fleming H. Revell Company, 1974.

# Other Good
# Harvest House Reading

### ROSES IN DECEMBER
by *Marilyn Heavilin*

Endorsed by Joni Eareckson Tada, God provides roses—special occasions, people, and memories—to help us through sorrow. Drawing from the loss of her children (crib death, pneumonia, drunk driver collision) Heavilin helps people deal with loss, understand grief, and find hope.

### THE QUIET HEART
by *June Masters Bacher*

In this devotional by June Masters Bacher, each daily devotional begins with a suggested Scripture reading, and through anecdotes, poetry, and prayer inspires each reader to see life with a fresh perspective. A day-by-day "friend" that encourages a quiet heart so you can come to know God and learn how much richer knowing Him makes each day.

### HOW TO WIN OVER WORRY
by *John Haggai*

People need help in overcoming worry and need it desperately. The worry problem is at the root of much domestic strife, business failure, economic crises, incurable sicknesses, and premature deaths—to mention but a few of worry's hazards. Presenting more than a diagnosis, Dr. Haggai shows how God's Word offers the prescription for worry that can rid us of the devastating effects of worry forever.

### STORMIE
by *Stormie Omartian*

The childhood of singer/songwriter Stormie Omartian, marred by physical and emotional abuse, led into teen and adult years filled with tragedy. Searching for an end to the inner turmoil which constantly confronted her, Stormie found herself on the verge of suicide. This poignant story gloriously reveals a God who can bring life out of death if we are willing to surrender to His ways.